NOT AS A CROCODILE

By the same author

LIFE WITH GROUCHO
THE ORDEAL OF
WILLIE BROWN

by
ARTHUR
MARX

NOT
AS A
CROCODILE

ILLUSTRATED BY GIL WALKER

HARPER & BROTHERS
Publishers, New York

TO THE MARXES AND THE KAHNS

CONTENTS

NOT AS A CROCODILE

1

The Immovable House Guests

My mother-in-law's house is a nice place to visit, but I wouldn't want to live there.

That's what I told my wife, and after nine years we moved out.

Actually, it didn't seem like nine years. It seemed like fifteen, but not because I wasn't very fond of my mother-in-law, or because we couldn't get along personally.

As a matter of fact, we had a lot of things in common—her daughter, for instance. And our literary tastes—we both liked to read the same part of the morning paper at the same time. And our love of the water—I was a sailor, and she had a swimming pool.

I'm not a sailor any more, but I was when I married Irene.

Ours was what you might call one of those hasty, spur-of-the-moment wartime marriages. Irene proposed to me when we were six years old, and fifteen years later, when I was a yeoman third class in the Coast Guard, I accepted her. We were married in February of 1943, when I was home on a two-day liberty.

Irene felt it would be too difficult for us to try setting up housekeeping while I was stationed aboard a ship. So she continued to live in her mother's house in Beverly Hills, and on the few occasions when I was home on leave, I stayed there, too.

It was to be a wartime expedient only, but when I was discharged from the service late in 1945, Irene still didn't want to leave her mother's abode. Southern California was in the throes of a housing shortage. Everybody was forced to double up—even movie actors and their wives were living together.

"It'll be a long time until we can find a place of our own," Irene explained to me. "So why don't the three of us just go on living here together for a while? There's plenty of room, and Mother would be delighted to have us. In fact, she's been coaxing me to stay."

To a fellow who'd been sharing a badly ventilated cabin meant for two with twelve other sweaty sailors, Irene's offer to live in a sixteen-room mansion complete with swimming pool had an irresistible appeal.

Besides, Grace Kahn was no ordinary mother-in-law. She may have looked the role—she was in her middle fifties at the time, and her hair was completely white—but she was younger at heart than either Irene or I, and her interests weren't confined to being a matriarch. She was a good homemaker and an accomplished hostess, but her heart was far from the kitchen—it was in Tin Pan Alley.

Grace's husband and Irene's father, the late Gus Kahn, had been one of America's best-known lyric writers. She'd helped him with his career, and she'd also had one of her own—as a piano player, song plugger and composer. With Gus she had written the big hit song of 1908, "I Wish I Had a Girl." She had retired to become a housewife shortly after that, but when I became her son-in-law she was still writing songs as an avocation—and getting them published and recorded by top artists.

"Okay, let's move in with your mother," I told Irene, "but only until the housing shortage is over. I don't think it's a healthy arrangement living with in-laws permanently. I read that in the *Woman's Home Journal.*"

"All right," agreed Irene. "Only until the housing shortage is over."

When Irene and I were getting ready for bed my first night home there came a knock on our door.

"Who is it?" I asked.

"It's me—Grace."

"What do you want?" asked Irene.

"I want you to hear my new song."

"But, Mother, it's after midnight. And Arthur and I—well, can't we hear it tomorrow?"

"I have to play it for Dinah Shore in the morning, and I want your opinion now, in case I have to change it."

"Oh, all right, we'll be right down," said Irene, putting on a robe and directing me to do the same. "Come on, dear, it will be simpler to hear it than to stand here arguing with Mother about it."

Grace sang the song for us in the living room, and accompanied herself on the piano. It was a very pretty ballad called "Dream a Little Longer."

"That's swell," said Irene when Grace was finished.

"I like it, too," I said. "Well, let's all go to bed."

"Do you think the first line of the bridge is all right?" asked Grace.

"It sounded all right to me," I said, recalling it only dimly.

"Let me play it for you again," said Grace. "I want to be sure it's right."

We had to hear it again—in fact, several more times. Then we spent about an hour reassuring Grace that the line was all right, and hinting that we would like to go to bed. By the time we returned to our room, it was one-thirty.

"Maybe we should get a place of our own," I told Irene. "I like to go to bed early. I don't think this is going to work out."

"I think it will," she replied, with a little laugh. "This doesn't go on every night—only some nights. But if you think we should move, then by all means, let's. After all, you're the boss."

Seven years later, in 1952, we were still living there. Only by then there were five of us, not including Irene's mother. In the intervening years we had acquired Steve, who was now five years old,

5

Andy, who was not quite a year, and Lucky, a mangy collie, who was four years old, and who bore considerable resemblance to Lassie, except in her earning capacity.

We were the kind of house guests to beware of: not only did we stay forever, but we multiplied.

Outwardly, our household appeared to be a very happy one. I used to overhear people say, "Isn't it remarkable how well the Marxes and Grace Kahn get along together? They'll probably never live apart."

"Why should they? Grace has her grandchildren right there in her own house, and the Marxes have Grace to run things for them. They've never had it so good."

Behind the scenes, however, things were quite different.

Grace liked having *us* there. But at least once a week, Irene would phone me at MGM, where I was working as a writer, and there would be a conversation like "We've got to move out, dear. I can't stand it here another day. Living with Mother is getting on my nerves."

"What is it this time?"

"We're losing control of our children. I just told Steve to take a nap, and he refused. He said, 'Nanny Grace says I don't have to.'"

"Well, that ought to be easy to straighten out. Just tell her about it."

"I have—hundreds of times. But it doesn't do any good. She goes right on spoiling Steve. So let's find a house and move out —right now."

"How can we move out right now? You can't find a house just like that."

"We can move to a motel until we find one."

"That's a little impractical, isn't it—with Steve and the baby and a dog? We've been there all this time. We can at least stay until we find a place."

"Okay, but let's start looking as soon as you come home."

This sort of dialogue had been going on for years, on MGM's time, with only the reason why we had to move being different. There were a number of reasons, and they were constantly cropping up. Some of the standard ones were:

(1) The children were getting out of hand living in the same house with their grandmother.

(2) Their grandmother was getting out of hand.

(3) Grace's second maid wasn't a good influence on Steve. She used to tell him frightening bedtime stories.

(4) Grace's piano playing was too loud.

(5) Grace was taking French lessons, and she had hired a French cook who spoke no English. We didn't mind not being able to tell her what we wanted for dinner, but we didn't like getting all our phone messages in French.

(6) Grace had taken up painting, and the place smelled of turpentine, and Steve was starting to play with matches.

(7) Grace did too much entertaining. If we wanted privacy, we had to hide in our bedroom.

In those days, Grace was sort of the Perle Mesta of the music business. Not only because she was basically a gregarious soul, but because entertaining is an important part of the music business. However, her own songs were only a minor concern. Her main business was promoting her husband's enormous catalogue of songs. As a result, our house was always filled with visiting music publishers, heads of record companies, singers, disk jockeys and song pluggers.

In addition, she was running a music publishing firm with Irene's brother Donald—the Gus Kahn Music Company—and they were using our house as its main headquarters. They weren't actually printing sheet music on the premises (although I wouldn't have been surprised if they had done that, too), but they were masterminding the operation from there. I was never surprised to come home from work and find some strange character from Tin Pan Alley demonstrating a song in the living room.

It was no place for a couple of introverts like Irene and myself.

But we never did start looking for a house, because, over the years, we had found just as many reasons why we couldn't leave:

(1) Irene was pregnant. It wouldn't be wise to move while she was in such a delicate condition.

7

(2) We'd gone to a great deal of expense making a nursery out of the bedroom next to ours, and you know how hard it is to find the *right* Mother Goose wallpaper.

(3) It was summer, and we liked the swimming pool.

(4) It was Christmas. It wouldn't be nice to leave Grace during the holiday season.

(5) We still hadn't used up our stationery with Grace's address printed on it.

(6) Grace was going to Europe, and we had to be her caretakers.

(7) Irene was pregnant again.

(8) We had just reordered more stationery.

And so it went, year after year. I was beginning to visualize myself still living there when I was an old man with grandchildren of my own—possibly even great-grandchildren—running around the house saying, "I can so look at *Dragnet* if I want. Nanny Grace says I can. And it's her television set. So there."

Then one day I met a movie producer who seemed vaguely interested in buying my first novel for a picture. I invited him to the house to dinner. We were going to discuss the project.

How did I know he was an old friend of Grace's from Chicago? They spent the entire evening discussing the good old days of the music business, when it was "really the music business."

"About my book," I started in on several occasions. But the producer was never listening.

"What ever happened to Mose Gumble?" he was asking Grace.

"He passed away."

"Too bad. He was a great guy. A real music man."

"Did I ever show you this picture of Gus and me right after we had our first hit? I was only seventeen, and it sold over a million copies."

Not only didn't this producer talk to me, except to ask me to get him a glass of water, but when the evening was over he had decided to make a movie of Grace and Gus Kahn's life.

8

"That wasn't very nice to do to Arthur," Irene scolded her mother the next morning. "That man was our guest. He came to the house to talk to Arthur about *his* book."

"Can I help it, dear, if he insisted on talking about Gus and me?"

"Well, you didn't do much to discourage him."

"I couldn't be rude."

"Well, it's pretty difficult to lead a life of our own here with that sort of thing going on. You know what, Mother? I think we ought to get a place of our own, if living here is going to interfere with Arthur's business. I don't think living with you is going to work out."

"You know what?" said Grace. "I've been thinking a lot about this lately, too. Maybe you two should have a little place of your own. After the picture's made, I'd like to do some traveling. I'll probably sell the house and move into an apartment, where I can stay when I'm in town."

"Oh, Mother, you don't have to move into an apartment," said Irene. "We'll keep a room for you in our new house."

Grace looked at us, horror-stricken. "Oh, no, I wouldn't do that," she exclaimed. "I couldn't stand living in somebody else's house!"

9

2

Disenchanted Mesa

Irene and I were a couple of pretty shrewd horse traders when it came to buying our first house. I guess that was the trouble. We were dealing in real estate, not horses.

However, when you consider that we'd spent nine years living with Grace, it's a surprising thing that we had enough independence left to be able to make up our own minds about any kind of a house. For that matter, it was a surprising thing that we were still married.

It had taken us a while to reach the stage where we were actually making offers on houses. We didn't let the real-estate agent rush us into buying the first house he showed us. It was the second house. I remember that distinctly, because the first house he showed us that Sunday afternoon that Irene and I and Steve and Andy and our dog went looking was much too expensive for our blood. It was about $5,000 more than he could possibly afford to spend. That's why he took us to the second house, because it was only about $10,000 more than we could possibly afford to spend.

Evidently he was trying to hoodwink us into buying the first house by using reverse psychology. But we fooled him. We liked the second house even better.

It was a seven-room California ranch-type bungalow, on a corner lot, with modern appliances galore, and it was in a brand-new subdivision in Pacific Palisades called Enchanted Mesa.

However, it was by no means perfect. It didn't have everything we were looking for, but then life is full of compromises.

For example, we wanted a house that was in a handy location. Well, this one was in a handy location—it was handy to the Pacific Ocean. On a clear day you could see the fog rolling in.

"Isn't it a little far out?" I asked the agent.

"Far from what?" he said, with a hollow laugh. And he had me there. Evidently word had already reached Pacific Palisades that I was no longer on the MGM payroll. Since I was free-lancing now—a euphemism for being out of work—I didn't have to drive anywhere to get to my business.

But since I was working at home, we also needed a house with a room in it that I could use as a study. This had a very attractive-looking den, with paneled walls and lots of bookshelves, and even a bar, in case I turned into one of those drinking writers. But it didn't seem very private to me, for in no matter what direction I turned, I found myself staring through a large opening into another room.

"It seems kind of open," I remarked to the agent.

"Nonsense," he said. "All you have to do is pull the sliding doors closed. And presto! A perfect writer's hideaway. Why, even I could write the great American novel in here, Mr. Marx."

It was a challenge I could hardly afford to turn down.

Another thing we needed was a house that was of Early American design, for we had been collecting antique furniture even while we were living with Irene's mother, and we wanted to be able to use it. But this house was ultra-modern inside, with large areas of sliding glass doors leading outside in most of the rooms, a brick wall at one end of the living room, a fireplace that was bizarrely off center, and nary a place for milk-glass bric-a-brac or planted garbage cans.

"It doesn't look very Early American to me," announced Irene when we were still casing the place. "What would we do with our antique furniture?"

"It would fit in like a charm," said the agent. "That's the advantage of buying a modern house. You can put Early American

11

furniture in a modern house, but you can't put modern furniture in one of those Early American eyesores. Just to show you what I mean, take a gander at that copper hood over the fireplace. That's definitely Early American in feel, yet the builder saw fit to combine it with modern décor."

"He probably had it left over from some other job," I remarked.

"Mr. Hatfield doesn't operate that way. He builds quality homes."

"I've always wanted a copper hood," said Irene, with a wistful sigh.

"Well, now's your chance to get one," said the agent. "Not many homes like this one left in Enchanted Mesa. And the prices of houses are going up and up and up."

Our fourth requirement was that the house have a nice back yard with a fence around it, so that our children and our collie would have a safe place to play. But the back yard to this place was nothing more than a vacant lot—an unfenced tangle of weeds and wild grass tall enough to conceal a good-sized lion. There were no trees, and it was littered with pieces of beaver board, scraps of wood, broken glass, empty paint cans and lumps of cement.

Evidently the builder had figured on hooking a couple of suckers just on the strength of how the place looked when you drove up to it from the front. Evidently he hadn't figured on locking horns with a couple of sharp-eyed operators such as my wife and me.

"Mr. Hatfield didn't do much with the back yard," I told the agent.

"Mr. Hatfield never does anything with the back yard," he replied. "That's his policy. He feels that back yards are a very personal thing. He couldn't possibly in a million years know what a potential buyer's landscaping requirements are. Just what did you have in mind?"

"I had in mind some grass with a fence around it."

"You can slap up a fence and plant some grass for a hundred bucks."

"The least he could do is take it off the price of the house," I said.

"It's already figured in the price," said the agent. "That's why it's being offered at such a ridiculously low price."

"I don't know," I said. "Maybe we should think it over."

"Don't think it over too long. There was another couple looking at the place just before you came. They were *more* than interested. They're going to bring their interior decorator back with them tomorrow."

"I think we should buy it," Irene said, taking me aside. "That copper hood's very attractive. And I'm sure that study will be quiet enough for you to work in."

"What about the yard?"

"You can fix it up yourself. I read all about how cheaply it can be done in an article in *House Wonderful*. And I'll help you."

Well, before you could say "twenty-year mortgage," the house was ours, we had moved in, and I was standing in the back yard with a hoe and a sickle and a number of other gardening tools I had picked up at Sears, Roebuck the day before. I was waiting for a representative of the Palisades Fence Company to appear and give me an estimate. I had been waiting for a week, and had finally decided I could be clearing away some of the weeds in the meantime.

My sickle and I had cleared away about a two-foot-square patch when I heard a rustling in the underbrush behind me. I turned to see Mr. Schwartzwald, who lives in back of us, walking toward me.

"Hi, neighbor," he said. "When are you going to put up the retaining wall?"

"What retaining wall?"

"The retaining wall between your property and mine. You've got about a ten-foot slope back there, and I don't want your drainage washing me out."

"That's not much of a slope," I said. "Besides, I'm putting up a fence—the man's coming out today—and the fence'll take care of it."

"That'll wash out, too," he said optimistically. "Besides, you can't put up your fence before you have the tractor man come in."

"What tractor man?"

"The one who's going to plow your lot under. If you're going to put a lawn in, and I presume you are, you have to plow up the weeds so they won't come up again, and level the whole thing off before your lawn man can come in."

"What lawn man?"

Schwartzwald looked at me disdainfully. "Certainly, Mr. Max, you're not going to put in a lawn yourself."

"The name's Marx. And I'm not planning on such a big project. I was figuring on landscaping my own yard. It's healthier. Besides, I can't afford to sink a lot of dough into the place at the moment. I just want an enclosed place for the kids to play."

"It'll be cheaper in the long run if you do it right to begin with," said Schwartzwald. "This place'll be a mess if you don't. The Enchanted Mesa Homeowners' Association won't like that a bit."

"Who are they?" I asked.

"That's the official organization of people who live in this area. I'm president. When you buy property here, you agree to abide by the rules. It's in your deed. And if you don't, we'll get after you."

"What if I refuse? What can the Homeowners do about it?"

"We can put a blemish on your title so you can't ever sell the house," he said in a neighborly tone. "And we have other ways, too."

I figured I'd better abide by the rules. I wouldn't want my kids to grow up knowing that their father had a blemish on his title, or that he had been lynched because he was too cheap to put in a retaining wall, or hire a lawn man. After all, what could it cost me? A hundred dollars? Three hundred dollars? Five hundred dollars? Seven hundred dollars and fifty-two cents?

If you guessed anything but the latter, you obviously have never had the pleasure of owning your own home. But that, of

course, included everything, even the redwood fence—a six-foot redwood fence so we would never have to see Mr. Schwartzwald again.

The whole project took six weeks. But don't think I was allowed to sit around idly during this time, writing a book. I had to supervise the whole operation, and make snap decisions that might affect my whole life.

How high did I want the retaining wall? What did I want it made of—bricks or cement blocks? How did I want the lot graded—level or slightly sloping? Did I want hose bibs? If so, did I want copper or iron pipe? Did I want the fence posts sunk in three or four feet of cement? Did I want Kentucky blue grass, or clover? Where did I want the flower beds? What kind of fertilizer? And did I know that the front lawn that Mr. Hatfield had put in was practically all crab grass, and what did I intend to do about it?

Nor was I merely answering questions while this was going on. I had to seal all the doors and windows of our house with rags so that the dust kicked up by the tractor wouldn't completely inundate us. I had to keep Steve from getting run over by the tractor, Andy from getting encased in one of the cement blocks used to plant the fence posts, Irene from selling our antiques and buying all modern furniture, and our collie from biting Mr. Otto, the lawn man. If anyone was going to bite Mr. Otto, I wanted to be the one, for he had run over our main water line with his harrow, and I had to get the plumber out on a Sunday (at fourteen dollars an hour) to keep us from having to take to life rafts.

While the plumber was there, he was nice enough to inform me that my water pressure was too high. "What you need, Mr. Marx, is a water-pressure regulator."

"Is it necessary?" I asked.

"Only if you don't want your pipes to burst. Too-high pressure also wears out your appliances. Every house should have a regulator."

"How come this one doesn't?"

"Spec house. Builder must have been cutting corners."

"This man wouldn't do that. He's a quality builder."

"Then maybe he just forgot."

"You don't have any idea where I could get a pressure regulator, do you?" I asked.

"I just happen to have one in my truck," he said. "Might as well do it now, as long as I'm out here. And I can let you have it for only sixty-five dollars, because it's last year's."

Obviously, it was going to save me a lot of money in the long run, so it was a lucky thing Mr. Otto had run over the pipe.

Finally, the lawn was planted, and I was standing in the back yard with Mr. Otto, looking over the newly seeded and fertilized ground.

"In three months it'll look like a putting green," said Mr. Otto.

"Is there anything I should do to make sure it comes up right?" I asked.

"Water it at least four times a day—keep it soaked so the sun doesn't burn up the young seeds. And don't walk on it for about three months."

"Anything else?"

"Well, could I have my check?"

After he'd gone, I stood there visualizing what the back yard would look like three months hence. In addition to a velvety green lawn, there would be magnificent fruit trees, climbing roses along the fence, flowers in the beds, a patch of vegetables perhaps, and a swing and a sandbox with children frolicking around them.

That's how I visualized it, but it didn't work out quite that way. Not that I didn't follow Mr. Otto's instructions to the letter. Every half hour, it seemed, I was rushing out to the back yard to water the new lawn. Then I'd return to my desk. No sooner was I buckling down to some serious writing than it was time to hose down the lawn again.

But the elation I felt when the first specks of green started to show through the fertilizer repaid me in full. I knew then how Balboa felt discovering the Pacific.

Unfortunately, about that time I made the mistake of looking at the front of the house. It was quite a shock to find that in my preoccupation with the back I had let the front get completely out of hand. The grass was nearly as tall as the baby elms, and the weeds in the geranium beds were so thick you couldn't find the geraniums.

I decided that if I didn't want the Enchanted Mesa Home-owners' Association to get after me, I'd better put my front yard in order. The planting in the back yard could wait until the grass grew up a little.

I promptly wheeled out my new lawn mower, and affixed the grass catcher to it.

"Let me help," Irene called to me from the front steps. "You promised I could do some gardening, too. I need the exercise."

She dashed into the house, and returned a few minutes later dressed in her new denim gardening outfit.

"Well, hand me some tools," she said. "I think I'll do some weeding. This place is a mess."

"What do you think I am, your butler? If you want to help with the gardening, surely you have the strength to walk to the tool shed."

"Oh, never mind. You can weed the flower beds," she said, grabbing the lawn mower. "I'm not much for weeding."

She wasn't much for mowing, either. It took her fifteen minutes to cut one swath through the knee-high grass.

"Well," she said, turning the mower back to me, "that's enough for the first day. I don't want to overdo it. Besides, I just remembered that I have to make the kitchen curtains."

I got her point—especially after I tried the mower. This mower wasn't built for such long grass, and neither was I. The grass kept clogging up the mower blades, and I had to stop every thirty seconds to untangle the mess and empty the grass catcher. While I was wondering if I should rip out the grass and put cement in, Glen, the part-time gardener from next door, meandered to a stop on the sidewalk.

"I guess you're going to be wanting a gardener now that you've got the back-yard lawn in, aren't you?" he asked.

"Nope," I said confidently. "I'm going to do it all myself."

He looked dubious. "My power mower could finish off that grass in a few minutes," he said.

"I enjoy the exercise," I said.

He shrugged. "I see your geranium beds need weeding. Ought to get after them now before they smother the flowers. Ground ought to be cultivated, too, if you expect anything to grow in this hard adobe."

"I'll get around to all that," I said. "In a month you won't recognize the place."

"Won't be able to see it," chuckled Glen. "Oh, well, if you ever need me, just holler."

"Don't count on it," I yelled to him as he walked away.

It took me three days to mow the lawn, including time out to have the mower repaired after I ran over a steak bone that Lucky had forgotten to bury. But that was child's play compared with weeding the geranium beds. The sun-baked ground was so hard you couldn't pull the weeds out. You had to dig them out one by one with a trowel.

Irene, of course, was still sewing curtains and pushing Early American dough boxes and cobblers' benches around in our modern living room, vainly trying to make the pieces look as if they belonged there. But Steve, being unoccupied, generously offered me his help in the garden, and I quickly accepted it. It was the only way I could keep him off the new grass in the back yard.

And, as a matter of fact, he learned pretty quickly for a five-year-old. He learned, for instance, that it was much easier to pull out the geraniums than the weeds. Before I realized what was happening, he had demolished seven geranium plants and proudly dumped them at my feet. "I'm a big help, aren't I, Daddy?"

"A very big help," I said. I was so angry I would have hit him over the head with a trowel, if I hadn't been too weak from the sun to lift it. Besides, my hands were blistered and it was time to water the back yard again.

But now we had a big bare spot which had to be utilized. Irene suggested rose bushes, so the next day found me at the nursery.

The attendant helped me pick out six beautiful rose bushes in full bloom, planted in tin cans. Each bush was labeled with a very impressive name, like Mother Machree's Baby Pink, or Isaac Gondorfer's Scarlet Pimpernel, and each one had garnered first prize at the National Flower Show. (Apparently flower shows don't give second or third prizes, for no matter what you buy at a nursery, it's always a first prize winner.)

In addition to rose bushes, my car, on the way home, was loaded down with sacks of fertilizer, bone meal, plant food, leaf mold, gallon cans of insect spray, a spray gun, tin snippers to get the bushes out of the cans, and a *Sunset Flower Manual*, which explained how to plant properly.

I couldn't have been better prepared if I were going to take up gardening as a profession. And judging from the amount of time I'd been able to devote to my book since buying the house, I'd soon *have* to take up gardening as a profession.

And I probably could make a pretty good living at it, at that, I figured as I dug the hole for the first rose bush. All you had to have was a little common sense and the right equipment, and know how to follow directions, and you couldn't go wrong.

Digging a hole was one thing. Getting a rose bush out of a can was quite another, especially since I'd been told that it would be fatal to the plant to let the dirt fall away from the root. Not only that, but at the first sign of the can's unwillingness to be cut in two, the tin snips fell apart in my hand.

"That was funny," said Steve. "Can I try it now?"

With a borrowed hatchet, I finally managed to mangle the can enough to try removing the bush from it. But as I picked up the bush, the dirt started to crumble away from its roots. My heart sank, but I managed to hold enough dirt together to get the bush over to the hole. But there wasn't any hole. Steve had filled it in when I was cutting up the tin can. Very tenderly, I set the bush down. As I did, the rest of the dirt fell away from its roots. Or rather, where the roots had been. The roots were gone, too. Apparently I had cut them off with the tin snippers and the hatchet.

In the days that followed I somehow managed to plant the five remaining rose bushes, and only once did I have to be taken to the emergency hospital for a tetanus shot, after I'd cut my hand on the rusty edge of a tin can.

Gardening wasn't quite so much fun as Irene, who was still busy as a beaver making curtains, had led me to believe. But it did keep a person from getting bored. The new rose bushes had to be watered, cultivated, sprayed and fertilized three times a week. The geranium bed I had weeded was beginning to sprout new weeds, the beds I hadn't yet got around to were beginning to resemble a jungle, and the front lawn was always in need of cutting.

In addition, I noticed one day that some disconcerting things were happening to the new lawn in back. All kinds of interesting-looking growths were popping through—devil grass, crab grass, wild radishes and wild oats. And if you looked closely enough you could even see some of the grass Mr. Otto had planted. But not very much of it, because the grass seed had blown over into the artistically designed spaces I had specified for flower beds and shrubbery, and had thrived remarkably well there. I could hardly find the flower beds.

I decided that I'd better stop beautifying the front for a while, and concentrate on the back yard. Of course, I still couldn't walk on the new lawn, but I could certainly begin planting shrubbery and fruit trees.

For a starter, the nursery man suggested camellia bushes, an orange and a lemon tree, and daisies, all planted in sturdy tin cans. And for an added fillip, he thought it would be a nice touch if I planted some zinnias and petunias. I didn't want to tackle too much at once, but after he informed me that both these varieties had won first prizes at the National Flower Show, I couldn't resist.

I must say that my experience in the front yard was a big help to me when it came to fixing up the back yard. The main thing it taught me was not to pull out the weeds one by one. In fact, it taught me not to pull them out at all. Why bother? New ones would just take their places. Leave them alone—let them smother each other, if they wanted. I couldn't care less. I had more important things to do. I could always get to the weeds later on in the summer, when I wasn't so busy.

The planting progressed nicely. With the new tin snips I had bought, the cans gave me no more trouble. I found the sunniest spot on the place—along the base of the house—and planted the camellia bushes there. It really dressed up the place.

I planted the orange and lemon trees near the kitchen window. This was a brilliant notion, too. As soon as the trees started bearing fruit, Irene could lean out of the window and pick off whatever fruit she needed for our meals.

But I've never been in better form than I was the day I put the zinnia and petunia plants in old Mother Earth. The plants were no larger than my fists. I planted four dozen of them in two hours, and I marked each one with a stick so I'd be able to tell the plants from the weeds. It was my most professional-looking job to date.

In two weeks the zinnias and petunias were about a foot high. I pictured all kinds of cut flowers around the house. But suddenly the zinnias and petunias took a mysterious turn for the worse. Their leaves were filled with Swiss-cheese-like holes.

"Snails," was the diagnosis made by the man at the nursery. "What you need are some snail pellets sprinkled around."

Snail pellets are about the size of sleeping pills, and they're made of arsenic. According to the nursery man, there's nothing better for getting rid of snails.

There's nothing better for getting rid of children, either. The pellets hadn't been on the ground twenty minutes before Irene and I were rushing Andy to the emergency hospital, after catching him in the garden gnawing on a suspicious-looking object. As it turned out, he had only eaten a snail, but Irene was pretty upset about it just the same.

"Don't you dare put any more arsenic in the garden," she said.

"What do you want me to do about the zinnias? Let them die?"

"It's better than poisoning your children."

"Who asked the children to go out in the garden?" I said. "The grass isn't ready to be walked on yet, or even cut."

Actually, it had been ready for a week, or at least as ready as it was ever going to get, but with a front and back yard planted, I just didn't have time for mowing two lawns, or even one lawn. I was spending all my time running back and forth between the two yards, watering the flowers and bushes, and spreading manure in strategic spots.

When I finally got around to mowing the back lawn, it did not resemble a putting green, as Mr. Otto had promised me it would. It looked more like the rough on a very tough golf course. The crab grass had overpowered Mr. Otto's grass and was slowly throttling it. And you couldn't even see the crab grass after our collie had spent an afternoon burrowing for gophers.

To make matters worse, the fruit trees were turning yellow, the camellia bushes were turning brown, and the rose bushes had lost all their leaves.

I took my problem to the nursery man, who informed me that I was giving the fruit trees too much water, that roses wouldn't grow in the shade, and that camellias wouldn't grow in the sun. It was easy not to give the fruit trees any more water. But transplanting camellias and roses was a man-sized job.

During the time it took me to do this, the weeds in both yards and on the street side of the back fence made considerable headway, without any help from me. I didn't spray them or fertilize them or even water them. They grew tall, anyway. And the aphids on the fruit trees, and the snails and the ants and the gophers, were all doing well, too.

Our little dream house was beginning to look like one of those decadent Southern mansions. Any day I expected to look out into the back yard and see Truman Capote lounging on a hammock.

All the neighbors were saying, "How do you like that Mr. Max? He buys a nice house and then he doesn't care about keeping it up."

"Well," I told Glen when I found him one morning, "I've changed my mind. I need a gardener, and I think you're the right man for the job."

"Too much work," he said, looking disdainfully at my yard.

"It would take me four months to get this place back in shape. I'd have to neglect my other customers."

I pleaded with him, even offered him ten dollars more a month than he was getting from anyone else, plus free lunches, but he couldn't have been less interested.

It took me two months to find a gardener who would accept the job. His name was Jim, and he was a very enterprising fellow. He was not afraid of working eight hours a day, or even nine. After I got my first bill from him, I understood why: he was charging by the hour.

But at least the garden was beginning to shape up. The fruit trees were looking healthy, the camellias and roses were flowering, the weeds were gone from the grass, and the bugs had been routed.

Irene and I were happy. Steve and Andy and our dog finally had a safe place to play, Irene could concentrate on making more curtains, and I could stay in the house and never set foot outside.

But when I went out to get the mail one morning, Jim buttonholed me.

"I'm quitting," he said. "Those kids of yours pull up all my pretty flowers, and that dog makes big brown spots on the lawn. All my hard work is for nothing."

"Kids will be kids," I said. "And collies will be collies. Don't worry about it. You're doing great."

"Either they go or I go," he said firmly.

Irene and I talked it over, and we decided that when you get an ultimatum like that, there's only one thing you can do. We enrolled Andy in Old Mother Hubbard's School for Tots, and Steve in the Comanche Boys' Club. We figured that would keep them out of the way until they were old enough to go to school.

As for Lucky, she's getting up a dog act and going into television with Lassie.

3

Schlempke versus Marx or The Case of the Slippery Washing-Machine Repairman

The old-style home, in which the husband works from sun to sun but woman's work is never done, is rapidly disappearing from the American scene. It has been supplanted by the mechanical household.

Perhaps you've seen illustrations of this home in the advertisements for household appliances in the *Woman's Home Journal* or *The Ladies' Companion*. The picture usually shows a beautiful housewife, immaculately dressed and smartly coiffured, standing in her gleaming kitchen, surrounded by a sink and garbage-disposal unit, a dishwasher, a washing machine, a clothes drier, a deep freeze, a stove that does everything automatically but season the food, and a refrigerator that not only dispenses ice cubes into highball glasses, but also makes the cubes out of seltzer or plain water.

"No more housekeeping worries for me," says the girl in the illustration.

Of course not! She isn't really a housewife at all. She's a model. If she were a housewife, she wouldn't have time to be standing around posing for pictures and making ridiculous statements. She'd either be on the phone, trying to get a repairman out to the house to fix the particular appliance that happened to break down that day, or else she'd be demanding that her husband do something about the situation himself.

In theory, there's nothing wrong with the idea of having automatic time- and labor-saving appliances do all the work for you. Irene and I were all for it, too. One look at our kitchen would verify that. We couldn't be better equipped if we were living in the home-appliance section of a department store. And I wish we were. The appliances in the department store are always in perfect condition, at least while the dapper salesman is giving you a demonstration and making his pitch. And usually these mechanical monsters will remain in pretty good working order for the first year you own them—provided, of course, you have a year's warranty of free service and defective-parts replacements from the manufacturer.

Oh, a few minor mechanical imperfections might turn up during the first twelve months—such as the dishwasher mangling a set of bone china, or the garbage disposal backing up into the guest bathroom the night you are throwing a housewarming party. But, by and large, you and your wife will be grateful for the labor-saving devices, and will frequently say to one another, "I don't see how we ever got along without them."

That's the way it was with us the first year. Irene and I passed many a cozy evening just sitting around saying, "I don't see how we ever got along without them."

Our troubles began the day our year's warranty on the clothes drier expired, for it was that day that the drier expired, too. The power was on—you could smell the motor burning—but the drum wouldn't revolve. Since it happened to be washday at the Marxes'— and a rainy one at that—Irene was stuck with a mountainous pile of wet clothes.

"I can't get the drier started," she said to me desperately. "You'd better come and look at it."

I looked at the lifeless machine for about fifteen minutes, giving it every kind of a look from a pleading one to a disapproving grimace. By then Irene and I both realized that just looking at it was getting us nowhere, so I took more direct action.

I phoned the Los Angeles office of the Major Electric Laundro-King Company, as our instruction booklet recommended, and talked to a surly man who promised to send a serviceman out by Monday.

"But this is only Tuesday!" I exclaimed. "And we have a whole houseful of wet wash. And we took our clothesline down."

"Monday," he said, and hung up.

Apparently I had said something that annoyed him, because he didn't send anyone out until a week from Wednesday. In the meantime, our wet laundry had been hanging from a temporary clothesline, and I had been walking around in a slightly damp shirt.

However, once the repairman did show up, it was only a matter of seconds before he had dismantled the back of the drier and had located the trouble—a rubber belt that was supposed to turn the drive shaft affixed to the revolving drum had merely slipped off its wheel. The repairman had only to slip the belt back into place on the wheel and the drier was as good as new.

It was such a relatively simple operation that we all had a good laugh. Why, if only I'd had the sense to look for the trouble myself, I could have put the belt back on the wheel, and this hard-working, kindly repairman would have been spared making the long automobile trip out to Pacific Palisades from downtown Los Angeles, and I would have been spared paying him eight dollars.

Nevertheless, it was a relief to pay him off and to get back to the book I was supposed to be writing. I had already wasted the whole morning watching the repairman, and I had to meet a deadline which was only two months away.

I had just typed out a whole word when a figure that looked very much like Irene appeared in the doorway and said, "Would you mind stopping what you're doing and coming out to the service porch? I think the belt has come off the drier again."

In the past, I would have been pretty disturbed by news of that nature. But knowing what I knew now, I realized that I could fix it myself. With a few turns of a screwdriver, I removed the back of the drier and slipped the belt back on the drive-shaft wheel. Then I turned on the motor, and presto, the machine started up. I was so pleased that I'd been able to cheat the Major Electric people out of an eight-dollar service call that I could hardly wait for the belt to come off the wheel again.

I didn't have to wait long. The belt slipped its wheel fifteen more times that afternoon. Running back and forth between my typewriter and the clothes drier kept me pretty busy, and I didn't get many pages written, but look at all the money I saved by not having to call a repairman. I figured it out, and it came to $128. That's pretty good pay for a day's work. If I could earn $128 every day, I could stop writing entirely.

In the next two months I put the belt back on the drier 147 more times, and theoretically earned myself a cool $1,176. By that time, I don't think there was a person in the world more skilled at putting a belt back on a clothes drier than I was. Unfortunately, this highly specialized talent was of little use to me the fateful day the drier stopped running for what must have been the 150th time.

The day dawned just like any other day—with Irene informing me that the drier had slipped its belt again, and would I please tear myself away from my typewriter long enough to put the belt back in place, so she could finish the laundry?

So you can imagine my surprise when, after I had dismantled the back of the drier, I peered in at the complicated-looking machinery and discovered that the belt was right in place. Everything, in fact, was right in place. The motor looked as good as it did the day we brought it home. But it wouldn't run.

"You need a new pump," was the diagnosis made by the repairman when he showed up six days later.

Not being an expert on pumps, I couldn't argue with him. I told him to put one in, if it was really necessary. But when he looked in his truck he discovered that he was all out of pumps. He'd have to pick one up at the main office.

Unfortunately, the main office was also out of new pumps— evidently there'd been a run on them—and they had to send my old pump into the factory in order to get a replacement. And the factory was in Trenton, New Jersey. These things I didn't discover until, at Irene's urging, I phoned up the main office ten days later to see what had become of my new pump.

"But don't you worry, Mr. Marx," the dealer assured me. "We think it'll be here soon."

Soon? We hadn't had any dry clothes in our house in sixteen days. And all he could make was some vague promise. I was really burning up.

"Well, I demand that you get out here TODAY and fix my drier," I shouted at him. "It's your responsibility. You took the pump out. If you can't get one from the factory, pick one up someplace else."

"There aren't any pumps around," he said. "You'll just have to wait your turn." And he hung up.

I was in no mood for waiting. I was tired of being pushed around by a group of incompetents. Surely in this age of jet planes and earth satellites there must be one appliance-repairing service that could fix a clothes drier—and one that was close enough so that they could get to my house on the same day I called them.

I thumbed through the local telephone directory, and sure enough, I found what I was looking for:

SCHLEMPKE'S APPLIANCE REPAIR SERVICE
Authorized Laundro-King Dealer

Schlempke was one of the friendliest and most co-operative fellows I've ever talked to. Not only that, but *he* had a pump for our machine. He had dozens of them, as a matter of fact. Of course, he'd have to charge me the full nine dollars, since I didn't have my old pump to trade in. But what did I care? He promised to be up himself within the hour, and that was good enough for me.

He was true to his word. Exactly one hour and a half later, the clothes drier was back in working order, and Irene was as happy as the girl in the ad and full of wonderful things to say about her husband, who had shown such ingenuity.

There was only one thing to mar our happiness that day. As Schlempke drove off, our Laundro-King washer stopped running.

Since Schlempke had done such an efficient job of repairing the drier, we got him back the next day to work his magic on our washing machine. And a good thing for us we had called Schlempke back, because by the time he arrived on the scene, the drier had broken down again.

There was very little wrong with the drier—just a couple of bolts that Schlempke had forgotten to fasten when he was putting the machine back together the previous day. He had that fixed after only an hour. But the washing machine—well, that was in very serious condition, according to Schlempke's diagnosis, and it probably wouldn't live unless we replaced its motor.

"How can it need a new motor already?" I asked. "Why, we haven't even finished paying for it."

"These things aren't built to last forever," shrugged Schlempke.

"But it's barely a year old," I protested.

"That's what I mean—these things aren't built to last forever," pointed out Schlempke, solemnly regarding the lifeless Laundro-King. "There just comes a time in the life of every washing machine when it needs a new motor."

"Well, if it needs a new motor, I guess it needs a new motor," I said philosophically. "How much will it cost installed?"

"A new motor costs forty-four fifty, and there'll probably be about eighteen dollars' worth of labor. But I wouldn't advise you to get a brand-new motor," Schlempke went on. "It's a waste of money. I can get you a new *rebuilt* motor for only twenty-seven dollars."

"Is a rebuilt motor any good?" I asked.

"Mr. Marx, would I sell you a bad motor? Believe me, it'll be like new. Besides, if you have any trouble with the motor, it has a year's guarantee."

Schlempke seemed like such an honest fellow that Irene and I questioned him no further. We told him to go ahead and install the new "rebuilt" motor. For only forty-five dollars, we couldn't afford *not* to have a washing machine that would be like "new."

The next day Schlempke arrived at our house with a new "rebuilt" motor, and spent the morning installing it in our washing machine. I'm no judge of motors, but it looked to me as good as a new one—at any rate, our friends would never know it was only a rebuilt one—and, what's more, it seemed to be in perfect working condition when Schlempke demonstrated it for us after he had finished installing it.

"There you are," said Schlempke, gathering up his tools and heading for the back door, "you can start in washing right now. I guarantee you you won't have a bit of trouble."

As Schlempke departed, Irene happily started loading up the washing machine with a couple of weeks' accumulation of dirty clothes. She couldn't wait to get at them with her new "rebuilt" equipment.

It was approximately noon when Schlempke drove away. At twelve-fifteen the washing machine started making a lot of disconcerting noises. At twelve-twenty it started to vibrate like a volcano about to erupt. At twelve-twenty-eight it began spitting oil and grease onto the linoleum and shooting streams of water out of its top, even though the door to the washing chamber was closed.

And at twelve-thirty it emitted a final convulsive rumble, and then collapsed into utter silence.

"I guess it needs adjusting," exclaimed Irene, making what I believed was the supreme understatement of the year.

We weren't able to get Schlempke out to the house any more that day, but he was back on our service porch first thing the next morning, giving our Laundro-King a thorough examination. I stood by, not worried—I knew Schlempke would stand behind his work—but interested.

"You know why it's leaking oil?" said Schlempke, finally emerging from behind the washing machine. "Your transmission's worn out. You need a new one."

"Wait a minute," I said. "You guaranteed this machine for a year."

He looked at me as if I were a small child. "No, I didn't," he explained. "I only guaranteed the *motor*. The transmission and

34

the motor are two different things. A transmission will set you back twenty-three fifty, without labor, of course, but I can get you a new *rebuilt* transmission for only—"

I had a feeling that Schlempke was playing us for a couple of suckers. I didn't even let him finish what he was saying. I handed him his tool kit, thanked him for his trouble and showed him to the door.

As soon as he was out of the house, I phoned the local office of the Laundro-King Company, and told them my troubles. They said they'd send a man out as soon as one was available.

Their man showed up at our back door exactly three weeks later.

By that time there was so much dirty laundry piled up in our service porch that there was hardly any room for the repairman to squeeze in. However, we finally managed to clear a space for him, and soon he had the washing machine dismantled and had located the difficulty.

"Darndest thing I've ever seen," said the repairman, shaking his head in disbelief, and looking at me accusingly. "Who's been working on this machine—you?"

"No—why?" I asked.

"Well, I wouldn't have believed it if I hadn't seen it," said the repairman. "This motor's in here backward!"

"Backward?" Irene and I both exclaimed simultaneously.

"Yeah—it's rotating the wrong way. That's why it's spitting oil and water."

"You mean there's nothing wrong with the transmission?"

"No. Who told you that?"

"The man who put in the new motor," I explained. "Schlempke —from Santa Monica."

"Well, he doesn't know what he's talking about," said the repairman. "It doesn't even look like a new motor to me."

"It wasn't supposed to be *brand* new," I explained.

"It's a brand-new *rebuilt* one," added Irene.

"It doesn't even look like a *rebuilt* one," replied the repairman. "It just looks like the one that was in here originally. Do you by

35

any chance know what the serial number was on the old one?"

"I don't even know my Social Security number."

"Then I guess you'll never know whether this is your original one or not. How much did he soak you?"

"The price he quoted us was twenty-seven dollars, without labor."

The Laundro-King repairman whistled in a way that told me we had been taken. "You could have got one from us for only sixteen dollars," he said. "And we would have put it in the *right* way. Boy, were you two robbed!"

Not quite!

We had come awfully close to being robbed, but fortunately we hadn't given Schlempke any money yet. We'd charged the work he had done, and he hadn't—as yet—sent us a bill. When I told this to the Laundro-King repairman, his advice to us was "Don't pay him. You're lucky he didn't wreck your whole machine. He ought to be reported to the Better Business Bureau. Probably wasn't anything much wrong with the old motor in the first place. He probably just fixed that."

We took his advice, and decided not to pay Schlempke's bill when it arrived in the mail.

It arrived on the first of the month—a bill from Schlempke's Appliance Repair Service for sixty-six dollars and fifty-seven cents.

I promptly filed it in the wastebasket, and waited to see what would happen.

A week later Schlempke sent me another bill, and, when I hadn't paid that by the twentieth of the month, I received a phone call from Schlempke himself.

"We're not going to pay you," I said boldly, and then I reeled off a pretty long list of reasons why I didn't feel I had to.

"If you don't pay me, you'll regret it," threatened Schlempke menacingly.

I leaned closer to Irene, who was standing nearby to give me moral support, and whispered, "He's pretty mad. Maybe we should pay him."

"What's he got to be mad about?" Irene shot back, grabbing

36

the phone from my hand. "Mr. Schlempke," she shouted into the phone, "if you don't stop dunning us, we're going to report you to the Better Business Bureau. You're not going to get any money from us, you crook, so you might as well face it."

She slammed down the receiver, saying, "That'll cool him off. We won't have any more trouble from Mr. Schlempke."

I returned to my desk, very much relieved that I had a wife strong enough to protect me from unscrupulous and unreasonable tradesmen. Undoubtedly she had frightened him away for good. He wouldn't dare risk our reporting him to the Better Business Bureau. All his shoddy business methods would be exposed. It would ruin his reputation for good.

Yes, that was undoubtedly the end of Schlempke—at least as far as we were concerned. It would be smooth sailing, or rather, smooth washing, from that point on, for both our washing machine and clothes drier were working perfectly now that the Laundro-King man had fixed them properly.

The phone conversation with Schlempke took place on Wednesday. On the following Monday I walked out to our mailbox—one of those RFD boxes at the curb—to see if a check I had been expecting from *Saga* magazine had arrived yet. There were no envelopes containing checks in the mailbox, but on the other hand there were no more bills from Schlempke, either, so I didn't feel too bad as I turned to go back inside the house.

As I started toward our front door, a Model-A Ford pulled into our driveway, and its driver, a nondescript fellow wearing a cap, said to me out of the corner of his mouth, "Are you Arthur Marx?"

"I am," I replied proudly.

"Greetings," he said, handing me an envelope.

As he drove off, I tore open the envelope, thinking how considerate it was of the MacFadden Publishing Company to be sending me my check by special delivery. But, as I quickly found out, it wasn't a special-delivery letter at all. The envelope contained an official-looking document that I knew, at first glance, was not going to add anything to our income.

SUBPOENA—CIVIL

In the Small Claims Court of Santa Monica

Plaintiff		Defendant
Joseph Schlempke	vs	Arthur Marx

Joseph Schlempke, being duly sworn, deposes and says that the Defendant is indebted to plaintiff in the sum of $66.57 for parts and labor on washer and drier.

You are hereby directed to appear and answer the within and foregoing claim, in the above entitled Court, Room 101, Santa Monica City Hall, December 31st, at 9 A.M.

Failure to appear will result in judgment being given against you in the above amount.

S. E. Hornsby
Clerk of Said Court

I was stunned. I was also a little disappointed in Schlempke. Not only was he an incompetent repairman, but he was turning out to be a poor sport as well.

"What's that you've got, dear?" Irene called to me gaily as I entered the front hall. "Did the check come?"

I showed her the subpoena.

"Why, that no-good so-and-so," muttered Irene. "What are you going to do?"

"I don't know," I said. "I suppose we ought to pay it and forget it—if he's that serious about collecting his money."

"Pay it?" exclaimed Irene. "I should say not. We have a good case against him. We'll fight it."

Before I could stop her, she had picked up the phone and was dialing our lawyer. "Two can play at this game," said Irene while she was waiting to be connected. "With Martin Gang defending us, Schlempke hasn't got a prayer."

Irene was right again. With Martin Gang defending us, Schlempke wouldn't have had a prayer. But, unfortunately, Martin Gang wasn't going to defend us. He was quick to inform us that you are not allowed to have the services of a lawyer in the small-claims court—at least not in California. You must defend yourself personally.

"But how can we win?" protested Irene. "We don't know anything about law."

"You don't have to know anything about law," explained Mr. Gang. "If you think you're justified in not paying him, just get all your facts together, and go down to the court and present them to the judge. Do you think you have a case?"

"Sure, we have a case," replied Irene. "We even have the repair bill from the Laundro-King Company, telling us that their man came out and found our washing-machine motor to be in backward. It's right there in black and white, in the repairman's own handwriting. Isn't that enough to show that Schlempke doesn't know what he's doing and that he tried to gyp us by sticking us with a new transmission which we didn't need?"

"It's probably enough," said Mr. Gang. "But unfortunately a handwritten notation like that doesn't carry any weight as evidence in court. I'd advise you to get the repairman out to testify on your behalf in person. Then you've got a case."

We had a case, but I didn't like the looks of it. After Irene hung up, I told her that I was in favor of calling the whole thing off and settling with Schlempke out of court.

"What on earth for?" asked Irene. "All you have to do is get the repairman out to testify and you'll win in a breeze."

"I don't want to have to stand up in court and look like a deadbeat in front of a lot of people," I said. "Why don't we just settle with him and be done with it?"

Irene regarded me with wifely contempt. "Are we so rich that we can afford to throw sixty-six dollars and fifty-seven cents down the drain?"

I was forced to admit that we weren't.

"All right, then," she said. "Get busy!"

Springing into action like Erle Stanley Gardner's energetic young D.A., I picked up the phone receiver. In a matter of seconds, I was connected with the man in charge of the service department of the Laundro-King Company.

"Hello," I said. "I want to speak to Bill."

"Bill who?"

"I don't know his last name," I said. "How many Bills do you have working there?"

"None that I know of," said the foreman. "We've got a Roy—"

"Get on the ball," I shouted. "A man named Bill came out to my house a couple of weeks ago from your company and fixed my washing machine."

"Oh, you mean Bill the mechanic," he said in an enlightened tone. "Sure, we have a Bill working here—I remember him now. But he's not here today. Roy's here, though. I can send him out."

"I don't want you to send anyone out," I said. "I just want to talk to Bill. I want him to be a witness for me in court in a couple of weeks. When will he be back?"

"He won't be back today. Why don't you call him tomorrow morning—before eight? Seven-thirty would be even better."

"Seven-thirty!? Can't I call him later?"

"You can, but he won't be here. He just comes in early and gets a list of the houses he has to go to, and then he leaves."

I called Bill at seven-thirty the next morning. But he hadn't come in yet. When I called back at seven-forty he'd already been there, picked up his list of calls for that day and departed.

When I finally reached him on the phone a week later, and explained the situation to him, Bill was most co-operative. "Sure, I'd like to testify for you, Mr. Marx," he said hesitantly, "but if I do that I'd lose a day's pay, and I can't afford that, especially right around the time when those Christmas bills will be coming in. Besides, we're kind of shorthanded around here, and I don't think my boss would let me go."

"But this is going to cost me a lot of money if I lose this case. And you're my star witness," I said. "Couldn't you just sneak away from work for a couple of hours without telling anybody?"

"I'm afraid of losing my job."

"Well, would you testify for me if I can get permission from your boss?" I asked. "And if he promises not to dock you?"

"Certainly, Mr. Marx. I'd be glad to."

I figured Bill's boss would be eager to expose a charlatan. After all, it would be good public relations for the company to help get a distressed owner of a Laundro-King automatic washer out of a jam. But the only thing Bill's boss was eager to do was get me off the phone.

"Sorry," he said after I had explained the situation to him in detail, "but we're not running a witness service. Bill's got more important things to do than spend a day in court."

"Well, if that's your attitude," I said, "I'm going to sell my Laundro-King equipment and buy from a more co-operative company."

What did he care? He was probably using some other company's merchandise himself. Either that, or he was making his wife do the laundry by hand, which is even smarter.

"Sorry—we'd like to help you, but it's a company policy," he said, and then he hung up.

I was pretty discouraged when I finished with him, and I was ready to abandon the case. But Irene wouldn't hear of it. "Would Clarence Darrow have given up so easily?" she said.

"Let's be sensible," I said. "How can we possibly win the case if we can't get Bill for a witness?"

"It's very simple," explained Irene. "Martin Gang told me what to do. You just go down to the courthouse and swear out a subpoena for this Bill whatever-his-name-is. Then he'll have to testify on your behalf whether he wants to or not."

It seemed like an amazingly simple solution to my problem. Why didn't I think of that myself, instead of wasting my valuable time trying to persuade these people to co-operate voluntarily?

Congratulating myself on having married a wife with such a steel-trap legal mind, and armed with Bill the repairman's complete name and address, which I managed to extract from his boss only after threatening legal action against his company, I marched into the marshal's office in the Santa Monica City Hall the next morning and announced that I wanted to subpoena a witness.

"What for?" asked the marshal, who looked just like an ordinary policeman to me, except that he was standing behind a counter.

"For my case," I announced. "Schlempke versus Marx."

"What's that?" he asked.

"My case!" I exclaimed, surprised that he hadn't heard of any impending legal action on the calendar as important as ours. "I'm being sued, but I'm going to fight it. I want to subpoena a witness."

The marshal, or at any rate this policeman who was posing as a marshal, slipped a blank subpoena into a broken-down typewriter and began filling in the required information as I gave it to him.

After the subpoena had been signed and notarized, the marshal started to give it back to me.

"I don't want it," I said. "I want it delivered."

"Delivered?" He seemed very much surprised. "You mean you want to hire a professional process server for a piddling case like this?"

"I'll thank you not to make light of my case," I said. "Yes, of course I want a process server. How else would I get it delivered?"

"You could serve it yourself."

"Way over in East Los Angeles?" I replied. "That's about forty miles from here. My time's more valuable than that."

He looked at me as if there was some doubt about my time being more valuable than that, and said, "It'll cost you some money if we do it."

"I don't care," I answered. "It'll be worth a couple of bucks to win this case."

"I'm afraid it's going to run you more than a couple of bucks," he chuckled, figuring with a pencil on a sheet of blank paper. "Process server gets thirty-five cents a mile, and it's ninety miles round trip to this man's house from here. That's about thirty-one dollars. Then there's the process server's fee—he gets two dollars an hour, and it'll take him about four hours, traffic being what it is these days, and whatever time he takes hanging around this fellow's house. And that's not even counting what you have to pay this witness for being a witness."

"You mean, *he* gets paid, too?" I asked.

"Certainly. Five dollars witness fee, plus mileage for him, plus what he loses by missing work that day. Altogether, it will run you about sixty-seven dollars if we don't run into any unforeseen difficulty, such as not being able to find the witness for a few days."

"Sixty-seven dollars," I exclaimed in dismay. "That's more than I'm being sued for."

"I know," said the marshal. "Sometimes it doesn't pay to get up in the morning, does it?" He laughed.

"Couldn't I just mail the subpoena to him?" I asked.

"Nope. Has to be handed to him in person," he said. "Otherwise it doesn't count."

"What else can I do?"

"Well, you could pay this Schlempke fellow the money you owe him. It might be simpler."

It was an idea all right, and one that appealed to me more and more as I drove home with Bill's subpoena tucked in my pocket.

"You know something?" I told Irene after I had explained the situation to her. "I think we ought to throw in the towel. No matter how this case comes out, we're going to be the losers."

"We could win if you weren't so lazy," she said.

"What do you mean by that?"

"I mean, why don't you drive over to this Bill's house and deliver the subpoena yourself? How much of your *valuable* time could it take?"

"It could very well take all day," I said. "And I don't happen to feel like hanging around in East Los Angeles by myself all day."

"Well," said Irene, her arms akimbo, "if you feel you can throw away sixty-six dollars and fifty-seven cents because you're too lazy to deliver the subpoena yourself, then don't come complaining to me the next time you think the grocery bills are too high. At least *I* try to *save* money."

Irene and I were heading for a showdown. Evidently the time had come for me to show her who was boss in our family.

"Okay," I said, "if that's the way you feel about it, I'll deliver the lousy subpoena myself."

Grabbing a rumpled fedora from the closet, I put it on and

pulled it down on my head as far as it would go so that Bill the repairman wouldn't be able to recognize me, in case he wished to avoid being served. And then I hopped in my car (cops and process servers never "get" in cars—they always hop in) and drove to East Los Angeles.

Normally, it takes about an hour and a half to get to East Los Angeles from where I live, but I used the new freeway, which is the way everyone travels these days, so it took me two hours. However, it was no fault of the freeway's. I merely took the wrong turn-off at one point, and wound up in Disneyland.

It was nearly two-thirty when I finally parked my car in front of a little white bungalow at 1296 Tortilla Avenue, which is the address Bill's boss had given me. But it didn't really matter that it had taken me so long to get there, because I knew Bill wouldn't return home from work until four-thirty of five, anyway.

My calculations were correct. At exactly five o'clock a car pulled into the driveway and a man got out. As he started up the walk toward the front door, I alighted from my car, subpoena in hand.

"Hi, Bill," I called to him breezily. "Can I see you for a minute?"

"Sure, you can see me," he said, "but my name's not Bill. My name's Edward Shufro."

"Isn't this 1296 Tortilla Avenue?" I asked. "I was told that a Mr. Bill Landow lives here."

"This is 1296 South Tortilla Avenue," he replied. "You're probably looking for North Tortilla."

When I arrived at 1296 North Tortilla Avenue, it was dark, and there were no lights on inside the house. I rang the bell, but no one came to the door. I figured Bill must have arrived home already, and then had taken the family out to dinner. I knew he had a family, because I had fallen over a tricycle on my way up the path.

I was getting hungry myself, but I decided to wait until Bill returned from dinner. There was no point in going home again, and having to return the next day.

But when Bill didn't arrive by midnight, I gave up and drove home, mission not accomplished.

As I trudged wearily in through the front door, Irene looked up from Jones' *Life and Work of Freud* (Volume 1) and said to me, "Well, you must have had a good time. You certainly stayed late enough."

If I hadn't been so annoyed at myself for having wasted the day waiting in front of the wrong house, I might have quit the case right then. But now I was determined to prove to Irene that I was capable of serving a subpoena.

I arose at five o'clock the next morning, and was parked in front of Bill Landow's house by seven. I felt sure that I had allowed myself plenty of leeway to catch the slippery devil on his way to work.

Evidently he was taking the day off, however, or else he had a private tunnel from his house to the Laundro-King Company, for no one came out of Bill's house between the time I arrived there and five in the afternoon.

Thinking perhaps they were all dead or something, I went to the house next door and inquired if the Landows were still their neighbors.

"Oh, yes," said the lady of the house, "but they're not there now. Mr. Landow decided to take his vacation at Christmastime this year. They won't be back until after the first of the year."

"Any idea where they went?" I asked, flashing my Junior FBI-man badge which I had found in my dish of cereal at breakfast that morning. "I have to get hold of them. It's very important, ma'am. It's quite a big case."

"Oh, I don't think you'll be able to reach them," she explained. "They went to the mountains. Mount Whitney. They're packing in."

As I wended my way homeward along the freeway, I decided I'd had enough. I wasn't going to turn mountain climber—for Irene or any other woman.

It's a wise man who knows when he's licked. And I knew I was licked—especially after I talked my problem over with Martin Gang that evening and he told me that, without a witness, I didn't have a chance. "Furthermore," he added, "you probably don't have much chance anyway. The court nearly always decides in favor of the plaintiff in these small-claims cases."

I phoned Mr. Schlempke as soon as his store was open in the morning and offered to settle with him for sixty dollars.

"Make it seventy," he said cagily, "and I'll accept."

"Seventy!" I exclaimed. "That's more than you are suing for."

"I know," answered Schlempke, "but this lawsuit has cost me a lot of money. Why, you wouldn't believe it if I told you how much those process servers get."

"No, and I don't want to know," I said, reaching for my checkbook.

4

The High Cost of Swordfish

There comes a time in every man's life when he needs a change of scenery—particularly if the scenery he's been looking at for the past six months has consisted mostly of the insides of a washing machine and clothes drier.

After my involvement with Schlempke, what I needed was a complete rest. My nerves were all shot. So was my bankroll. I kept having nightmares about washing machines, and according to Irene, I woke up every night screaming, "I am not a deadbeat, Your Honor. Schlempke's a crook!"

The situation definitely called for a vacation—and a cheap one, at that.

I was in that frame of mind when a friend of mine named Charlie Isaacs called on me one evening. Charlie is an ardent fisherman. He's caught tuna off South America, smoked salmon off Nova Scotia, pneumonia off Alaska, and marlin off Guaymas, Mexico. And he has a bloodstained fishing cap to prove it.

Somehow the discussion got around to vacations, and when Charlie learned that I was in the market for one his face lit up and he exclaimed, "I could use a few days off myself. How about you and me going to Catalina this weekend, and we'll do some swordfishing? That's real sport."

Until then, my piscatorial experience had consisted chiefly of taking Steve to one of those trout ponds where you are permitted to catch fish that are so tame they practically line up in the water for the privilege of being hooked by anyone willing to pay a dollar apiece for them. But I must confess that I'd been nurturing a secret yen to catch something more exciting ever since I'd seen my first picture in a magazine of Ernest Hemingway swordfishing off the coast of Cuba in his private yacht.

It had occurred to me at the time that probably the main difference between Hemingway's writing and mine was that I didn't do enough swordfishing. And as the years went on and he won the Nobel Prize, and I didn't, I was sure of it. But I was deterred from taking up swordfishing myself, because it was obviously a rich man's sport—reserved for people who owned their own yachts. I barely owned my own car.

So when Charlie Isaacs suggested we go swordfishing, I naturally protested that I couldn't afford it.

"Nonsense," said Charlie. "Anybody can afford it. We can charter a private boat at Catalina for only fifty bucks a day, with all the equipment thrown in, and we'll split the cost. You can afford twenty-five bucks, can't you?"

There it was, as simple as that: a chance to be Ernest Hemingway and to get away from the family—for only twenty-five dollars. A man would be a fool to turn down a proposition like that.

And I'm no fool—at least I didn't think so at the time.

"Well, if we're going away I'll have to buy some new clothes," announced Irene.

"And I need some swimming trunks," said Steve.

Charlie frowned. "Doris and my son are going to stay home," he informed us. "If there's one place I refuse to take Doris and Ricky, it's on a fishing trip!"

Since Charlie felt that way, there was nothing I could do but put my foot down and suggest to Irene that she and Steve stay home, too, and perhaps get together with Charlie's wife and son for some kind of an outing.

Fortunately for me, Irene's a very understanding wife. And if she resented my attitude, she no longer showed it by Friday night when she, Steve and I were holed up in a room at the St. Catherine Hotel on Catalina Island.

By then I already had a substantial investment in the swordfish I was planning to catch. There were the new beach outfits for Irene and Steve; the boat fares over to the island from the mainland; baby-sitting fees for the lady who was taking care of Andy at home; and, of course, what it was costing us to stay at the hotel. Thirty-six dollars a day for a room that overlooked the gardener's tool shed.

The only cheerful note was that Irene and Steve, and Doris and Ricky had promised not to interfere with our fishing. They were going to stay behind and take in the sights, Irene having heard that no visitor to Catalina Island could afford to miss the exciting rides on the glass-bottom boats, and Wrigley's Bird Farm.

Charlie was up at five Saturday morning, knocking frantically on our door.

"For Heaven's sakes—hurry!" he shouted as I groped for my clothes in the dark. "The swordfish are starting to jump. I could see them breaking water from my room."

The boat Charlie had hired was a thirty-five-foot power craft called The Restless. She had once been white, but by now most of her paint had peeled off, and she smelled of dead fish.

The skipper, a weather-beaten old sea dog (who also smelled of dead fish), was revving up the engine when we arrived on the dock.

"You the guys who aim to catch a swordfish?" he asked, glancing rather contemptuously at my store-crisp blue denim outfit and Charlie's bloodstained fishing cap.

We nodded eagerly, and the skipper motioned us aboard.

As The Restless headed for the open sea, Charlie and I stood on her stern and waved good-by to our families. Our families, however, were unable to wave back, for they were still in their hotel rooms, sound asleep.

"Nothing like the salt air to make you feel good," Charlie shouted over the roar of the motor. "As soon as I set foot in a boat, I forget all my worries. How about you?"

"I feel good, too," I said, filling my lungs with exhaust fumes. Sleepy though I was, I must admit that it was quite a thrill for me to hear the skipper announce a little while later that we were in "swordfish waters." I jumped up eagerly from my swivel chair on the stern and reached for the deep-sea fishing rod that had been assigned to me.

"I'll bait your hook for you," offered Charlie, reaching into a bucket and bringing out a dead flying fish. "Swordfish are just about the smartest things that swim. If you don't bait your hook just right, you might just as well have stayed home in bed."

Grateful for such a friend, I watched Charlie insert the huge hook in the back of the flying fish and toss it into the sea.

"Let out about seventy-five yards of line," Charlie advised me, "and then put your clicker on. When a fish strikes, your reel will sing out and the skipper will stop the boat. Then count to ten, throw on your drag to set the hook, and start reeling her in."

My blood tingled with the excitement of the expected catch as I sat there tilted back in my chair, with the blue sky overhead and a staunch boat beneath me—to say nothing of a bucketful of dead flying fish that were beginning to smell.

I was ready!

But the swordfish was not.

About eleven o'clock Charlie decided that maybe he had put the bait on the hook the wrong way. We reeled in, changed the position of the flying fish on the hooks, and let our lines out again.

By one o'clock we had forsaken fresh bait in favor of trolling with feathers. And by midafternoon Charlie was convinced that the skipper was at fault. The arcs he was making with the boat weren't large enough, and he was trolling too slowly.

Charlie took over the helm personally.

But by five o'clock, when we were heading back to the dock, the closest we had come to a fish was the tuna sandwich I had brought along for lunch. I was tired, sunburned, discouraged and a little angry with myself for having wasted the money.

"It wasn't wasted," said Charlie philosophically. "Chalk it up to experience. Tomorrow we'll make up for it."

"Tomorrow?"

"Certainly. You want to try it again, don't you? You can't go back to Pacific Palisades empty-handed—a failure. What'll your friends think?"

I hadn't looked at it in quite that way before, but I could see his point.

At dinner that evening, when Charlie and I announced that we were planning on taking *The Restless* out again the following day, our wives exchanged disapproving glances.

"Well, I'm not going back to that bird farm again," insisted Irene. "When you've seen one bird, you've seen them all."

"And that goes double for glass-bottom boats," Doris remarked bitterly.

If we didn't catch any swordfish Sunday morning, it wasn't because fishing conditions weren't ideal—or that we weren't fully equipped.

The girls, who had made it known beforehand that they were coming along only for the boat ride, were amply supplied with sandwiches, fried chicken, thermos jugs of coffee, the latest reading matter and lots of sun-tan oil. And Steve had brought along his Space Patrol rocket gun—a harmless little toy that expels a rubber-tipped missile capable of putting your eye out if you are within range (and on a small fishing craft, you are always within range).

As soon as the sun came out, the girls stripped down to their bathing suits, found a comfortable place on the bow—away from the children—and spent the morning applying sun-tan oil to each other's shoulders.

That left it squarely up to Charlie and me to keep the waves, which were larger than the previous day, from washing Steve and Ricky overboard, and to prevent them from maiming one another, and us, with the rocket gun.

I couldn't help feeling that it was never like that when Ernest Hemingway took to the open sea.

The lunch, I have to admit, was delicious; and afterward Charlie and I returned to our rods with new hope.

It was around that time Steve sidled up to me, his face a sort of hunter-green color, and said, "I don't feel so good, Daddy."

Irene must have suspected what was wrong with Steve, for without a word from me she let out a scream, scrambled down from the bow, and rushed Steve over to the side of the boat—and just in time.

"I wish you'd tell your family not to make so much noise," complained Charlie. "They're scaring away all the fish."

The Restless, meanwhile, was living up to her name. She was lurching uncomfortably from side to side, and her deck was slippery with spray.

"Arthur!" It was Irene's voice, and she was furious. "Will you please put down that rod and come over and help me? Can't you see that *your* son is seasick? I can't hold him up to the railing much longer. He's heavy!"

"Yes, dear," I said obediently, and I started to reel in my line. As I did, I felt a jolt on the other end of it that nearly pulled me over the stern, and my clicker sang out noisily.

That I had actually hooked a swordfish never occurred to me. "I guess I've snagged some seaweed," I told Charlie. "Will you get it off the hook for me? I'd better go help Irene."

I started to hand him my pole, but he drew back.

"Are you crazy, man?" he shouted at the top of his lungs. "You've got a strike!"

All hell broke loose as my reel continued to unwind at a merry clip. The skipper cut the engine and came running to the stern with a gaff, with Doris and Ricky close at his heels. And in the background I could hear Steve groaning, and Irene threatening to divorce me if I didn't come at once.

Under the circumstances, I made the only decision I could. I told Charlie that he'd have to land the swordfish for me. But before I could protest, he and the skipper had strapped me securely into my swivel chair and were shouting instructions at me.

"Throw on your drag," said Charlie. "And don't get excited. Just do as I say."

What could I do? I threw on my drag. My heavy rod bowed almost to the breaking point as the swordfish's frenzied leaps carried him in and out of the water. (Actually, I'm not sure that it was a "him" at all; it could just as easily have been a "her.")

For thirty minutes, with Charlie screaming advice into my ear, I doggedly wound and unwound my reel. My hands were blistered, my arms ached, and I could hardly hold on to the rod. But the swordfish seemed farther from the boat than ever.

"Charlie," I finally gasped. "Take my rod and you play him for a while. I can't go on."

Charlie looked at me scornfully. "It's not sporting to alternate, and don't ever let me hear you say anything like that again!"

"Take it for a minute," I pleaded. "No one'll ever know."

"I'd know," replied Charlie, walking away.

Somehow I managed to stick it out; and an hour and fifty-five minutes later I had the glassy-eyed monster alongside the boat. The skipper gaffed him, put a steel cable under his tail, and hauled him on board.

"Congratulations!" said Charlie, flinging his arms around me. "That beauty must weigh at least two-fifty."

"Biggest one of the season," said the skipper.

"Can I feel him?" asked Steve.

Steve had recovered by this time, and was gnawing on a piece of fried chicken. But Irene was sulking on a bench amidships and chose to ignore both me and my swordfish. She thought I had deliberately hooked him to avoid my fatherly duties.

"What do you say we call Catalina on the ship-to-shore phone," Charlie suggested to me, "and notify them of our catch?"

"It's traditional," added the skipper.

"Then do it—by all means," I said enthusiastically.

It wasn't until after he had completed the call that the skipper made it known that there was an extra five-dollar charge for all ship-to-shore messages.

As *The Restless* headed for home, with her swordfish pennant flying in the breeze, the skipper turned to me and asked, "Mr. Marx, what do you want to do with your fish?"

This was something I hadn't thought of. "Well, I don't know," I replied. "What do you suggest?"

"I'd have him stuffed and mounted if I were you. He's a beauty."

I agreed that it was a good idea.

"I know a place on the island where you can get it done for seventy-five cents a pound," said the skipper. handing me a business card.

It didn't taken any Einstein to figure out that getting this fish stuffed would cost me somewhere in the neighborhood of two hundred dollars. For that price I could get a genuine reproduction of a Grandma Moses to hang over our fireplace instead.

"I don't want to spend that much," I said. "What else can I do with him?"

"You can eat him."

"I don't like fish."

"Neither do I," said Charlie quickly, as though he were afraid I might offer the fish to him.

"Can't we sell him?" I asked the skipper.

"Mr. Marx," said the skipper, his feelings obviously hurt, "this is a sporting boat. We're not allowed to sell fish commercially."

"Then you keep him," I said generously.

"I don't want him."

I tried to remember what Hemingway did with his swordfish, but I couldn't recall ever reading about how he handled that problem.

"Then let's throw him overboard," I finally suggested.

Again the skipper looked at me coldly. "That's against the fish-and-game laws. Five-hundred-dollar fine if they catch you. I won't be a party to it—might lose my boat operator's license. Besides, there's a thousand-buck reward for anyone reporting such a violation. Never can tell who might talk."

I got his point. I also consented to let his friend stuff my fish. What was the use of going to all the trouble of catching a swordfish if you couldn't hang him up in your house and show him off to your friends?

On the dock, a crowd awaited *The Restless*. Since mine was the only swordfish caught that day, our ship-to-shore message had been relayed all over the island.

As my fish was hoisted up on a block and tackle for the islanders to admire, a young man ran over to me and said, "Mr. Marx, I'm the official photographer. You want your picture taken with the fish, don't you? It's only two dollars a picture."

I recognized a bargain when I heard one. That was cheap compared with my other expenses. "Okay, I'll take one," I said.

"It's three for five dollars," he informed me. "I don't print less than three."

I had to go through with it. He'd already set up his camera and tripod, and Irene and Steve and the Isaacs were all grouped around me and the fish.

The moment the photographer snapped the shutter, a group of anxious spectators, all carrying their own cameras, pushed us aside and promptly proceeded to take pictures of themselves standing beside *my* swordfish.

As we disentangled ourselves from the mob, another very effusive gentleman rushed up to me and shook my weary hand.

"Mr. Marx, congratulations! You're now a member in good standing of the Tuna Club."

"I am?" I said, wide eyed. "I never thought I'd make it."

"Well, you did indeed." He handed me an application blank. "And if you'll just fill this in and send us a check for twenty dollars, you can be a *lifetime* member!"

My fame as a fisherman had already preceded me to the hotel. An announcement on the lobby bulletin board stated:

ARTHUR MARX—SWORDFISH—237 POUNDS—TWO HOURS, 25 MINUTES

While Irene and I were studying this, about a hundred and fifty hotel guests, in a festive mood, descended upon us and literally forced us into the cocktail lounge. There, for the next two hours, everyone, including the bellboys, hotel clerks and chambermaids, drank to my health.

There's no use in denying it; I was quite proud of myself. And

Irene must have been impressed too, for when she spoke to me after that, it was in a friendlier tone.

Almost as friendly a tone, in fact, as the bartender used when he handed me a bill at the end of the evening for $89.68.

"I thought this was on the house," I protested.

The bartender favored me with a solicitous smile. "It's customary, Mr. Marx, for the man who catches the fish to treat everyone."

"Pay it," advised Charlie. "Don't ruin a wonderful day by being a cheapskate."

One afternoon, about a month later, my stuffed swordfish arrived at our house in a large crate. Wishing to surprise Irene, I unpacked the fish and hung it over the mantel.

"Heavens, no—get that fish down immediately," said Irene the moment she saw the new decoration. "I won't have that frightening thing spoiling the looks of this room now that I've finally got it fixed halfway decently. It just doesn't fit."

And in a way she was right. We still had our Early American furniture, and this wasn't an Early American swordfish.

"Well, what do you suggest I do with it?" I asked. "It cost me a fortune to catch it, and I'm not throwing it away now."

"Then we'll just have to build on a playroom or den," she suggested. "You know—the kind of a place where you can hang hunting and fishing trophies. I saw a wonderful room like that in some magazine. It belonged to some famous writer—I think it was Ernest Hemingway."

5

Not as a Crocodile

I've always considered myself a model father, so it therefore came as quite a shock to me when I discovered that Steve, who was now six, thought I was a crocodile.

Of course, he didn't come right out and call me a crocodile, but that's what the psychiatrist said he was thinking. And who am I to question a psychiatrist?

The whole thing started one Sunday afternoon when, at Steve's request, I gave up my regular Sunday-afternoon golf game to take him to see the movie *Peter Pan*. After saying good-by to Irene and Andy, Steve and I set out for the Pantages Theater in Hollywood, where the movie was being shown at one of those kiddy matinees.

Steve and I arrived at the theater in plenty of time to nail down two good seats, but already the air in the place was oppressive with the odor of rancid melted butter, and there was a heavy blanket of spilled popcorn on the floor. It looked like an old-fashioned white Christmas in Vermont.

During the running of the movie, I could hardly hear the dialogue because there was so much bubble gum snapping all around me. And at frequent intervals I was hit in the back of the neck by a cold stream of water that was being fired at me by some unidentified assailant who had brought a water pistol to the matinee.

But I consoled myself with the thought that those are the

sacrifices you have to make if you expect to go on enjoying the love and respect of your children. And since it was obvious that Steve was having a good time, I couldn't complain too much.

In fact, when it was all over, I was rather proud of myself for having been such a doting father that afternoon.

Irene said she was proud of me, too, that night when we were getting ready for bed. "You should have heard Steve telling me about the wonderful time you two men had at the picture by yourselves," she added. "I'll bet *you* had fun too—probably more fun than you would have had cursing your way around the golf course."

"I never curse on the golf course," I grumbled.

"You know what I mean," said Irene. "You had a good time today—I can tell. Didn't you?"

"Yes—great," I replied, thinking of how cold the water from that squirt gun had felt on my neck. "But next week I think I'll force myself to play golf. I need the exercise."

As we got into bed, and I reached up to turn off the lamp, a blood-chilling shriek pierced the air.

"My goodness—what's that?" exclaimed Irene, jumping out of bed and into her robe and slippers.

"It sounds like Steve," I said, following her into the hall.

When we arrived in Steve's room, he was sitting up in bed, the light from the hall illuminating his face, and he appeared to be extremely frightened.

"I'm scared," he cried, as Irene put her arms around him comfortingly.

"Of what?" we asked, genuinely surprised, for up until this point in his life, Steve had never shown any indication of being a nervous sleeper.

"Of the crocodile," he blurted out. "One was chasing me."

"That's absurd," I said. "There are no crocodiles around here."

"Yes, there are," insisted Steve. "There's one under the bed right now."

I looked under the bed, just to make sure that some crocodile hadn't put one over on me, but there was nothing there except an empty cereal box and some toys that had been lost for about a month.

Then it suddenly dawned on me that Steve was having a delayed reaction from seeing the crocodile in *Peter Pan*. Irene was of a similar opinion, so the two of us sat down on the edge of Steve's bed and together we tried to allay his fears.

First of all, we pointed out, he couldn't have been chased by a crocodile, because he was still in his bed; he must have dreamed about it. Secondly, there couldn't be a crocodile anywhere in the neighborhood, because the Enchanted Mesa Homeowners' Association wouldn't permit it. Thirdly, even if there were a real crocodile in the neighborhood, how could he get into our house without a key? And lastly, there are no crocodiles in Southern California; they are all in the swamps of Florida and Louisiana.

"That's not true," sobbed Steve. "What about the crocodile we saw this afternoon in the movie? *He* wasn't in Florida."

"He was just a make-believe crocodile, dear," said Irene in a soothing voice.

"If he was only a make-believe crocodile," asked Steve skeptically, "how could he bite off Captain Hook's hand?"

"Captain Hook isn't real either," I explained. "Some cartoonist at Walt Disney's studio drew him. Captain Hook's an animated cartoon—just like the bad old crocodile."

"What's an animated cartoon?" asked Steve.

It's not easy to explain the mechanics of cartoon animation to a six-year-old at one in the morning (especially when you're not sure yourself), but it was either that or stay up the rest of the night holding Steve's hand. So I plunged into a detailed account of how cartoons are made.

When I finished my long, technical and, I'm sure, inaccurate explanation of the mechanics of cartoon animation, I asked Steve, "Now do you understand about the crocodile?"

"Yes," he answered, "but I'm still scared." He started to get out of bed. "I want to get in *your* bed."

"In our bed?" I exclaimed. "What on earth are you afraid of now? Didn't I explain to you all about how cartoons are made? How silly can you be?"

"I'm scared," said Steve. "I want to sleep with you. Please, can I?"

"Oh, stop being a baby," I roared, "and go back to sleep— in your OWN ROOM!"

"Arthur!" said Irene. "Please don't talk to Steve that way. Can't you see the poor boy is frightened to death?" She turned to Steve, saying, "Of course you can get in bed with us, darling. Come right ahead." And taking him by the hand, she led him into our room, where he crawled into bed with us.

Before long, Steve was sleeping peacefully. So was Irene. But I tossed and turned the whole night through. I just couldn't get comfortable on that narrow strip of mattress that had been allotted to "Daddy."

I was deeply grateful when day finally broke, and Steve apparently reassured by the cheerful sunlight, voluntarily left the security of our bed and trotted blithely back to his own room.

I was pretty sleepy at work that day, but at least the experience of the night before had taught us an invaluable lesson in child raising. There would be no more kiddy matinees or scary movies for Steve until he was a lot older. Apparently movies were too stimulating for him.

I was doubly convinced of this when Steve's nightmare, in which the same crocodile was chasing him, came back Monday night for a return engagement. Again, Irene and I tried to quiet his fears by pointing out to him how utterly impossible it would be for a crocodile to be inside our house, but Steve wouldn't listen to anything reasonable. The only thing that had a calming effect on him was Irene's offer to share our bed with him again that night.

I didn't exactly relish the idea of spending a second night balancing myself on the edge of the bed, and to make matters even more crowded, Steve brought his Teddy bear to bed with us—one of those giant, almost life-size, Teddy bears. But as I said earlier, with parenthood, you must resign yourself to making certain sacrifices, so I didn't fight it.

However, when the same thing happened five nights in a row, I began thinking that perhaps Steve needed less comforting and more a good clouting. He was, in my opinion, overdoing a good thing. How long could a person—even a six-year-old—go on being frightened by the same crocodile?

I was in favor of being firm with Steve. "If he tries it again tonight," I said to Irene on the sixth morning, "I think we should tell him to turn around and march right back to his own room."

"I don't think that's a very sensible solution," said Irene. "That's not going to stop those horrid nightmares."

"If you have a better solution, let's hear it."

"Well," said Irene, "I was talking with Jean Maxwell yesterday, and—Did you know, dear, that she and Jonas have been taking Billy to a child psychiatrist ever since he bit his piano teacher?"

"I've heard the teacher play, and I don't blame Billy," I said.

"No, I'm serious," said Irene. "Jean says the psychiatrist has done wonders for Billy. Maybe somebody like that could help Steve stop having nightmares."

"Oh, no," I said. "My son's no case for a head shrinker. He just got frightened by a scary movie, and it'll take him a while to get over it. It's as simple as that."

"Well, that's not what Dr. Freeman thought."

"Who's Dr. Freeman?"

"He's Billy Maxwell's psychiatrist."

"You mean you talked to him behind my back?" I was furious.

"It isn't behind your back. I'm telling you right now. I made an appointment to see him this afternoon. Why don't you come along?"

"I don't need to," I said scornfully. "I can stay right here and tell you exactly what he'll tell you. He'll say: 'Don't take your son to any more movies with crocodiles in them.' It doesn't take a psychiatrist to figure that one out."

As obvious as the case seemed to me, I could see that Irene

wasn't going to be satisfied until she had sought the advice of an expert. So I told her to go ahead and consult Dr. Freeman, if it would make her feel any better.

I could hardly wait for Irene to return home from Dr. Freeman's office late that afternoon, and tell me that he had confirmed my own diagnosis of the case.

"Well, what did old Dr. Freud have to say for himself?" I asked the minute Irene walked in the front door. "I'll bet he agreed with me, didn't he?"

Irene flashed me a rather peculiar smile, and suggested that we'd better repair to the solitude of my study before discussing the matter any further.

"What's all the secrecy about?" I asked, as I closed the study door behind us.

"I'm afraid you're not going to be pleased," she began hesitantly.

"You mean, I'm not going to be able to take Steve to any more kiddy matinees? Why, I'm heartbroken."

Irene fortified herself with a deep breath, looked at me pityingly and said, "Dr. Freeman doesn't believe the movie has very much to do with Steve's nightmares. He says the picture just acted as a trigger mechanism that set off symptoms of some deep-seated psychological problems that are disturbing him."

"Would you remind repeating that?"

"Well, according to Dr. Freeman," said Irene, "Steve is going through the Oedipus stage. This is the age where he is in love with his mother, and he sees you as a rival for my affections."

"What that got to do with crocodiles?"

"It's very simple. In Steve's dreams, the crocodile is merely a personification of his father. It isn't a crocodile he's afraid of—it's you!"

"Me?" I couldn't believe my ears. "Are you trying to tell me that Steve thinks I'm a crocodile?" I said explosively. "Is that what that quack told you? Why, that's absurd. Why should Steve be afraid of me? Why—I've been nothing but nice to him ever since he was born. Why—I used to change his diapers. I used

to get up with him in the middle of the night and give him his bottle. Why—why—why, I even took him to the movies last week. How could be possibly think *I'm* a crocodile?"

"Calm down, dear—calm down," said Irene patiently. "It has nothing to do with how nice you've been to him. All boys go through this stage where they love their mothers and have feelings of hostility toward their fathers."

"Tommyrot!" I snorted. "Why couldn't Steve just be afraid of crocodiles? If you ask me, it's perfectly normal to be afraid of crocodiles. They're vicious-looking animals. I'm afraid of them myself."

"Well, you're probably harboring some latent feelings of hostility toward your own father," suggested Irene.

"Ridiculous!" I said. "If the movie didn't have something to do with it, why is Steve suddenly dreaming about crocodiles? He didn't have any feelings of hostility toward me *before* last Sunday?"

"The crocodile is only a symbol," explained Irene. "It just so happens that you took him to see *Peter Pan* when he was on the verge of this Oedipus stage. It was just a coincidence. If he hadn't seen *Peter Pan* he might have started having nightmares about some other animal—a lion or a tiger perhaps."

"I still don't believe it," I said. "And furthermore, I think it's pretty damn conceited of you to tell me that you think *our* son is in love with you and considers me a rival."

"I'm not conceited," said Irene, starting to walk away. "And if you just want to be stubborn, I'm not even going to discuss it with you."

"Discuss it?" I said. "What's there to discuss? It's all cut and dried according to you. Steve is crazy about you and hates me. Do you want me to move out of the house now, or can I wait until after dinner?"

"I hate sarcasm," said Irene.

"Well, I hate psychiatrists who go around making rash statements about people they haven't even met," I retorted. "That's the trouble with psychiatry—it's full of psychiatrists who go around making rash statements."

"Psychiatry could be a big help in getting rid of Steve's nightmares—if only you'd co-operate," she said, raising her voice.

"How much more can I co-operate? I just offered to move out of the house, didn't I?"

"Don't be funny," replied Irene, "and listen to what the doctor said to do. It makes a lot of sense."

"Oh, no," I said suspiciously. "*I'm* not going to go to a psychiatrist."

"Nobody has to go to a psychiatrist," said Irene. "All we have to do, he told me, is change our attitude toward Steve. In other words, you have to do more to make him like you, and I have to do less. For instance, if he does something naughty, let me do the punishing. That way he'll take all his resentment out on me, and he'll regard you as a nice fellow."

"What else did he have to say?" I asked skeptically.

"He said you and Steve should get off by yourselves and have a good time together—don't even take Andy with you. Go to the movies, and—"

"I took him to the movies—that's how all this started."

"Yes, and that was the first time you'd missed your golf game and spent a Sunday with him all summer. The doctor says you should take Steve out more often. Buy him presents. Just bend over backward being nice to him. And above all, when he tries to get in bed with us at night, don't yell at him and try to stop him. Make him perfectly welcome. That way he won't think of you as a rival, because you won't be standing in his way of being with his mother."

"But I've always been nice to him," I protested. "He doesn't even appreciate it."

"You'll just have to be nicer, and pretty soon he won't be thinking you're a crocodile."

"How awfully decent of him."

"Let's not be bitter. Let's just try what the doctor recommended. Maybe it'll do some good."

I said I'd give it a try, though I still didn't believe the theory, and just to prove that there weren't any hard feelings, I took Irene in my arms. As I did, the door flew open and into the room walked Steve. He looked rather disapprovingly at what we were doing, and then, pushing me aside, he put his arms around Irene and said, "I love you, Mommy."

I studied him in amazement, this cherub-faced, towheaded boy, who was barely three feet tall with his shoes on. It was hard to imagine him the third person in a tempestuous triangle—two men fighting for the love of one woman, and all that.

Still, there wasn't much doubt of the truth of it any longer. I had no choice but to do as the doctor ordered.

The next eight weeks were devoted chiefly to making Steve think of his father not as a crocodile. We were together constantly.

I took him to so many kiddy matinees that I could tell you exactly how many kernels there are in a bag of popcorn (86 in the ten-cent size, and 153 in the large economy box), and how many times an average healthy child can kick the back of the seat in the row in front of him (53).

I indulged in a vigorous athletic program with Steve. Of course, he was too young for golf—even for caddying—but I taught him baseball and touch football, and he taught me Kick-the-Can and Chinese handball.

I showered Steve with presents, and raised his allowance from five cents to six cents a week, so he wouldn't have to be beholden to me for chocolate-cigarette money. I even gave him a subscription to *Playboy* magazine. (He couldn't read yet, but I didn't mind reading it aloud to him.)

And lastly, and probably most important, I didn't do any punishing, nor did I speak any harsh words to Steve, no matter how much his behavior warranted it. Whenever he was especially naughty, like the day he punched Andy, I simply turned the case over to Irene. She would see to it that he got his just deserts.

It was an excellent system that Dr. Freeman had recommended. Irene was the disciplinarian, and I was the amiable social director. There was just one thing wrong with the system: the situation wasn't improving any. Steve was still getting up regularly in the middle of every night and wanting to come in our bed with that ridiculous Teddy bear. Apparently, in spite of my efforts, he still thought I was a crocodile.

It was discouraging, to say the least. What's more, I was getting eyestrain from seeing so many movies, my golf clubs were getting rusty from inactivity—and so was my golf game—and I had nightly insomnia from sleeping three in a bed—or four, counting the Teddy bear.

"I'm sick of this nonsense," I finally said to Irene one morning after a sleepless night. "We've got to do something."

"Don't get excited," advised Irene. "Dr. Freeman told me not to expect any overnight miracles."

"Overnight miracles!" I said. "It's been eight weeks. If you ask me, you ought to call up that quack and ask for our money back."

"Just be patient," said Irene. "I'm sure we ought to see some results pretty soon now."

I didn't tell Irene, but I decided that *I'd* been patient long enough, and that the time had come for action.

I was awake and waiting for him when Steve came tiptoeing into our room at a quarter past twelve that night.

"Daddy, there's a—"

"Out!" I roared, sitting up in bed and pointing to the door. "Don't give me that crocodile routine. Go back to your room and go to sleep."

"Arthur, that's no way to talk to our son," said Irene. "Can't you see he's frightened?"

"Frightened, my eye."

"Yes, he is. And yelling at him is no way to reassure him."

"He doesn't need reassuring," I said, jumping out of bed. "What he needs is a good sound spanking."

"Nobody is going to spank this poor defenseless child—you big bully," said Irene, putting her arm around Steve protectively. "Why, he'd be traumatized for life."

"Maybe so," I replied, "but I'll bet he wouldn't have any more uncontrollable nightmares."

"Spanking is definitely not the way to handle the situation," said Irene with authority. "And Dr. Freeman wouldn't think so, either."

"Then let *Dr. Freeman* sleep three in a bed, and see how *he* likes it," I told her. "As for me, I've had enough."

With that, I picked up my pillow and headed for the door, saying, "I hope you two will be very happy together. I'm going to sleep in the living room."

"If that's the way you feel about it, you don't have to come back," Irene called to me.

As I stumbled down the darkened hall on my way to the living room, I heard Irene slam the bedroom door.

Being a father's for the birds, I thought to myself as I settled down on the sofa for the night. It's idiotic—the whole chain of events just doesn't make sense.

One day you're a happily married husband and father, and the next thing you know you're a crocodile sleeping on the living-room couch.

Well, that's life and you can have it, I thought as I turned out the light and tried to get comfortable.

I had just changed positions for what must have been the thirty-second time when I saw a shadowy figure steal into the room and over to where I was lying. He was short, and wearing Dr. Denton pajamas.

"Daddy," said Steve in a loud whisper.

"What do you want?" I asked.

"I want to keep you company."

"You want to keep me company?" I raised myself up on one elbow and looked at him incredulously. "Go keep your *Mommy* company."

"I don't want to keep Mommy company."

"Why not?"

"Cause she's not nice."

"What's wrong with her?"

"She's mean. She called you a big bully, and you're not a big bully."

71

I was stunned. "You mean you like me?"

"Sure, I like you. You're the best daddy ever. You take me places, and we have a keen time together, and—"

"Okay, okay," I said, trying to take this encomium calmly.

It was heartwarming having this vote of confidence after what I'd been through, and it certainly didn't sound like the statement of a child who hated his father. That Dr. Freeman—what a fake! He must have got his degree from a barber college.

"Come with me," I said, leading Steve down the hall.

I marched into our bedroom triumphantly, and turned the light on. Irene sat up, and I could tell she hadn't been asleep.

"You know what?" I announced. "You and that horse doctor have got this thing all backward. I don't believe this kid thinks I'm a crocodile—I think he thinks *you're* a crocodile."

"What gave you that brilliant idea?"

"Steve just told me I'm the greatest daddy in the world, and he thinks you're mean. What do you think of that? And what do you think of your big theory now?"

Irene looked at me and started to laugh.

"What's so funny?" I asked.

"You. It's all so obvious, and you can't even see it. I think the theory is a hundred per cent correct. Of course Steve likes you. And why do you thing he likes you? Because we've been following Dr. Freeman's advice, and for the last two months you've been paying some attention to Steve instead of running around the golf course every chance you get."

"I don't believe it. I don't think he *ever* hated me. And I don't think that's why he has nightmares. If that theory is so great, why doesn't he stop having nightmares now that he likes me? How come he had one tonight?"

"But I didn't have a nightmare tonight," interrupted Steve.

"You didn't? That's wonderful!" exclaimed Irene.

"Well, if he didn't have a nightmare, what was he doing in our room?" I asked.

"I just came in to tell you about the mouse," Steve said.

"Mouse?" Irene jumped up on the bed. "What mouse?"

"The one that woke me up. I heard a noise and I went in the bathroom and there was a mouse."

"I may faint," cried Irene. "He's probably running all over the house by now."

"No, he isn't," said Steve. "I shut the bathroom door on him. He's still in there. I just heard him squeaking."

"Now I know I'm going to faint," said Irene.

That's about all there is to the story. I cornered the mouse, there were no more nightmares and no more nightly visits to our room by Steve.

But one day, several years later, when Andy was approaching the Oedipus age, he came to me and said, "Daddy, will you take me to see *Peter Pan*? It's playing at the Bay Theater."

"I'm afraid not," I replied. "*Peter Pan* is much too scary for small children. It might give you bad dreams."

"You took Steve to see it," Andy reminded me.

"Well, I'm not taking *you*," I said. "And that's final."

You can imagine my dismay when Andy said to me a few weeks later, "Guess what, Daddy? You don't have to take me to see *Peter Pan*. It's going to be on television."

Perhaps I shouldn't have let this frighten me, but on the weekend *Peter Pan* was scheduled to turn up in our living room, I took four of the main tubes out of our television set and hid them in my closet. Being a crocodile once in a lifetime is enough for me.

6

Those Wild Hollywood Parties

I once attended a cocktail party at a very fashionable home in Spring Lake, New Jersey. Before it broke up, three guests had passed out from too much champagne, one man pushed another fellow, who was fully clothed, into the swimming pool, and an overanxious suitor ripped off his girl friend's skirt. In the midst of all this, the host, a very dignified, gray-haired gentleman, knowing I was from Hollywood, turned to me with a rather pleased expression and remarked, "Say, this is turning into a regular Hollywood party."

He didn't get a chance to delve any deeper into the subject, for he, too, passed out shortly after making that remark, but the implication was clear enough. What he meant was that the average Hollywood party must be a good deal wilder than the wildest party held in other sections of the country. Not because of the geographical location or the semitropical climate (although there is a school that believes that smog acts as an aphrodisiac), but simply because Hollywood parties are attended by people who work in movies, radio and television, and who are, as a result, much more sinful than ordinary people.

It isn't surprising that most people have this impression of Hollywood parties—not when you consider that they get the bulk of their information from Hollywood gossip columnists.

A sampling from one of the columns, following a big weekend

74

in movieland, tends to make the Roman orgies of Nero's day look pretty tame in comparison:

"All Hollywood turned out Saturday night for Gloria Harrison and Tony Taylor's sixth anniversary party. Couple were celebrating six whole months of wedded bliss. . . . Party was a divine idea—a circus motif—and Gloria and Tony had their back yard decorated to resemble Barnum and Bailey's big top, which was the real thing, incidentally. The big top was loaned to them by John Ringling himself, who was passing through Beverly Hills on his way to Sarasota, and he just happened to have his tent with him. . . . For a gag, Rod Hunter arrived on an elephant which he had flown over from the Belgian Congo especially for this party. . . . Producer Willie Korngold got a little too frisky after his thirteenth martini and rode his motorcycle off the diving board into the swimming pool. Everyone, especially Willie, had a good howl when it turned out that Gloria and Tony had emptied the pool for the winter. Poor Willie! Guess he'll have to stop drinking martinis, if he can't hold them any better than that. . . . The guests who attended are still wondering where calendar girl Marilyn Stone and host Tony Taylor sneaked off to in the middle of the proceedings. And for why! They didn't return to the party for nearly two hours. Naughty, naughty, Tony. And at your own anniversary party . . . Better keep an eye on hubby, Gloria. . . . Or is all forgiven after he gave you that forty-thousand-dollar Black Mist mink stole? . . . And to top everything off, making the party one huge success, at midnight nude girls—nude, that is, except for a coating of luminous paint—were shot out of cannons into the waiting arms of those bachelors who were asked not to bring dates because no more leaves could be put into the main dining table."

That sort of thing makes for a very readable column, but what I want to know is: where do you find such an affair, and what do you have to do to get invited to it?

I wouldn't want to disillusion anybody, but I've been living in Hollywood since I was six years old and I've never yet been to a party where anything sexier than puffed rice was shot out of a cannon.

So what? you're probably saying to yourself. What does that prove? Nothing, except that Arthur Marx is a social outcast who just doesn't get invited to the right places.

Well, that's not exactly true. It's partly true: I *am* a social outcast. But in Hollywood, even social outcasts get invited to parties. And over the years I've been to enough different kinds of blowouts in movieland, even including that *crème de la crème* of Hollywood social functions, the tent party, to be able to say, and with some authority, that the wild Hollywood party is a complete myth.

The Tent Party, at which, if anywhere, you might reasonably expect the oats of that myth to be sown, is so named because your host and hostess have invited not only more people than will fit into their dining room, but more than will fit into their whole house. The result of such slipshod managing is that they have to go out and rent a small-size (or one-ring) circus tent in which to house the party, and have it erected in their back yard. Tents for this purpose are not hard to find in Hollywood, but they are costly. Luckily, the tent is a deductible item, and so are the tables and chairs and silverware, which also have to be rented.

As a matter of fact, about the only thing that doesn't have to be rented for the evening are the guests. In Hollywood, guests are as easy to come by as oranges and palm trees. Just pick up a phone and call somebody, and you have a guest. All over Hollywood, producers, directors, actors, actresses, writers, composers and singers are sitting by their phones, waiting and hoping to be invited to something resembling even slightly the proverbial wild Hollywood party.

The Tent Party, of course, has all the earmarks of a wild Hollywood party, and each time you are invited to one you are ever hopeful—long before the big night—that it will turn into an evening of debauchery.

You can tell beforehand that it's going to be a tent party simply by driving past your host and hostess' house a couple of days prior to the event. If there is a truck from Abbey Rents pulled into their driveway and at least a fifty-foot tentpole protruding into the air from their back yard, you'll know that your host and hostess are planning to lay it on pretty thick.

That's how it happened the last time Irene and I were invited to what turned out to be an important party at the home of Mr. and Mrs. Walter Culhane, the producer of that tremendous Technicolor musical in Cineramascope, A Yank on the Left Bank.

As we drove by the Culhanes' house one afternoon and noticed the truck from Abbey Rents, Irene touched my arm and said in an excited voice, "I didn't know the Culhanes were going to have a tent party. Now I have to buy a new dress."

"What for?" I said. "What's the matter with the dress you bought for the last party?"

"You're just like all husbands," said Irene. "You want your wife to look lousy at these affairs. But if you get a chance, you'll probably be off in a corner with some starlet who's wearing a three-hundred-dollar dress cut down to here."

She pointed to "here," and I must confess that I wasn't totally disinterested in the prospect of getting together in a corner with this hypothetical creature. And I don't think my feigned indifference to the matter fooled Irene for a moment, either, because by the time the party rolled around, she, too, was sporting a brand-new dress, and also a brand new thirty-five-dollar permanent.

However, Irene needn't have worried so about me winding up in the corner with some vampire.

In the first place, it's extremely difficult to corner a starlet at a tent party, because most of the tents are round and—well, they just don't have any corners.

And secondly, there never seems to be an overabundance of glamour girls at any of these affairs. And the ones that do turn up belong to the A group and flatly refuse to have anything to do with run-of-the-mill guests like the Marxes.

The A Group, as distinguished from the B, C and D Groups, consists of people who have at least one of the following qualifications:

(1) A long-term contract at a major picture studio
(2) An Oscar
(3) A foreign sports car
(4) A 29.3 or over Trendex rating on television
(5) A wife (or husband) who has (1), (2), (3) or (4)

The B and C Groups consist of an assortment of Hollywood characters in various stages of success, and the D Group consists mostly of the host and hostess' relatives and perhaps a couple of neighbors who happened to stray too far from their own house and accidentally got swept up in the descending throng of invited guests.

Irene and I have a B-minus standing, which is about the best a magazine writer can hope for, so after our hostess greeted us at the entrance and introduced us to a couple of people who belong to the A Group—just to show us how democratic she was—she shunted us over to the bar. Not the A Group bar, which was on the other side of the tent, I later discovered, and where they were serving imported champagne, but the B Group bar, where 76-proof whisky was flowing like water, and tasted like it.

There Irene and I found ourselves trapped between Sam Salkow's wife, who looks less like Marilyn Monroe than Sam Salkow does, and the host's sister-in-law, Mrs. Fitzpatrick, who bore a startling resemblance to W. C. Fields. Where Sam Salkow and Mr. Fitzpatrick had disappeared to I'll never know, but I didn't blame them.

As she reached for another chicken liver wrapped in bacon, Mrs. Salkow proudly announced to me that she had just taken up painting, and at the same moment Mrs. Fitzpatrick ecstatically announced to Irene, "I'm in analysis!"

Three drinks later, Mrs. Salkow had all but convinced me that I had a great deal of natural ability as an artist and should take up painting so I could illustrate my own articles, and Mrs. Fitzpatrick had all but convinced Irene that I needed to be psychoanalyzed. (Evidently Irene had told her about how I had resisted taking Dr. Freeman's advice in regard to Steve and the crocodile.

78

And anybody who resists is automatically suspect, they both agreed.)

At this point I began to realize that if anything wild was going to take place at this party, it was not going to occur anywhere in the vicinity of Mrs. Salkow and Mrs. Fitzpatrick and the rest of the misfits who were standing around the B Group bar.

So with drink in hand, and Irene hanging on my arm, I set off in search of some excitement. I looked high and low for it—I even mixed in with the A Group by pretending to be one of them—but the most lively thing I could find before dinner was an argument between two producers about whether or not a certain actor at the party was wearing a whole toupee or just a "frontpiece."

Luckily, I didn't have to wait to hear how the argument turned out, because just then Irene thought she noticed some signs of activity down at the other end of the tent where the caterers had set up their steam tables, and she started dragging me in that direction, exclaiming, "Let's be the first in line. I think we're going to eat soon."

Since it was nine-thirty already, that seemed like a reasonable assumption. But after we stepped to the head of the line and had selected our plates and silverware, we discovered that the only food in sight was a huge tureen of clear broth, which turned out to be the hot water for the steam table.

"Dinner will be ready shortly," said the austere-looking caterer, noticing our hungry glances. "Why don't you help yourselves to some hors d'oeuvres in the meantime?"

It was an old trick, filling the guests up on hors d'oeuvres so they wouldn't want very much of the main course, but we refused to fall for it.

Forty-five minutes later, when dinner was finally unveiled, I wished I had fallen for it.

It was the same dinner the same caterer had served in the same tuxedo in the same rented tent at every party I'd been to in Hollywood in the past five years: beef Stroganoff (probably made

79

of scraps of meat left over from one of Dore Schary's parties), noodles in a ring, cauliflower au gratin with green peas around it, lime Jello-mold salad, rolls, ice-cream slices and lukewarm coffee. It was the seventy-five-cent blue-plate special at Clinton's Cafeteria, except that the coffee was colder.

But if the dinner was uninspired, at least the dining table I had my eye on for Irene and me looked promising. Sitting at it, with two vacant seats beside her, was Maria St. Maria, the voluptuous brunette whom our host had imported from Italy to star in his latest picture.

"Let's sit here," I told Irene as I put my plateful of Stroganoff down beside Maria St. Maria.

As I started to leap into my chair, I felt a tug at my elbow and, turning around, I found myself face to face with our hostess. "Would you and your wife mind terribly—?" she said, indicating another choice table fifty feet away behind a tentpole. "The photographer from *Life* is here and he wants *us* all together. It's easier for him to take pictures that way."

"Us" obviously meant the A Group. And it was then, as I watched the photographer starting to shoot Maria St. Maria from all angles, that I found the answer to a question about Hollywood parties that had been bothering me for many years: Why do the B, C, and D Groups get invited at all? Answer: So there will be enough people in the background of the publicity pictures to make it look like a large and important party.

In other words, the B, C, and D Groups are sort of like "dress extras," only they get paid in beef Stroganoff instead of folding green stuff.

Eating dinner without Maria St. Maria wasn't too unendurable —after all, I'd done it on other occasions and survived. What I really minded was the table where Irene and I finally ended up. Not only was it behind a tentpole, but it was up against a flaming-hot, portable kerosene heater used for getting the chill off the place. Every time I moved my legs, I scorched my pants. And I had to do plenty of moving, for our table was adjacent to one of the main thoroughfares to the dance floor. Whenever the band started playing, I had to leave my chair and stand up against the heater to let the dancers by. It was either that or crawl under the table. And there were too many legs under the table to make this practical—especially since none of the legs were worth looking at.

Believe me, the only thing that prevented me from grabbing Irene and leaving for home was the thought of all that revelry I would miss after dinner, when things would begin to get wild. I wanted to be sure to be around when they started driving motorcycles off diving boards and shooting naked girls out of cannons.

But somehow—perhaps the merrymakers were tipped off that I was there—the orgy never got started.

Oh, there was extemporaneous entertainment, all right. Phil Shimpkin, the television comedian, tried out his monologue for next week's show on the guests; Frank Gruskin, the song writer, played a medley of his latest hit tunes; dancer Gene Riley, who showed up at the party in the same pair of blue jeans he's worn since winning an Oscar last year, did his most requested dance number, "The Old Soft Shoe"; and Abe Barrow, who devotes his life to writing specialty songs, such as "The Girl With the Four Green Eyes," for parties, played his newest, "The Girl with the Five Green Eyes," and was screamingly funny.

By then it was nearly eleven-thirty, and Maria St. Maria was beginning to yawn and look sleepy. "My goodness, it's getting late," she told the hostess. "I have to run. I have a nine-o'clock call on the set."

The rest of the A Group soon followed suit, for they had jobs and had to get up early, too. In fact, the only people who stayed on real late and had a wild time were Irene and I.

We were there until four in the morning, trying to find our car that the boy who ran the parking concession had misplaced in some alley.

However, I haven't entirely despaired of finding a wild Hollywood party. I don't know where it's going to be, but I have a pretty good idea when it will take place—in about fifteen years. That's how long it'll take a certain group of characters I know to grow up into the kind of guests who can really make a party jump.

I met this group recently, when I had to take Steve to a birthday party in Beverly Hills, given by Judy, the nine-year-old daughter of an important movie and television comedian whom I shall call Red Gordon. I hadn't been invited officially. I simply made the mistake of letting my automobile engine die when I was dropping Steve off at the front door of the Gordons' ultra-modern hilltop home. Before I could make my getaway, the Gordons spied me and insisted that I stay for "a hamburger and a piece of birthday cake."

It was strictly an A Group birthday party. There was a swimming pool on the premises (not just *a* swimming pool but a shamrock-shaped swimming pool), and a projection room for thirty-five-millimeter movies in the house. The boys and girls were culled from some of the most important movie and television business families in the neighborhood, and how Steve came to be invited I'll never know.

The party got off to a rousing good start during the swimming session before lunch, when three nine-year-old boys were caught peeking into the girls' dressing room, which was plainly marked "For Mermaids."

"We were just trying to find the bathroom," one of the peeping Toms explained.

A likely story. But since no one could prove otherwise, the charges were dropped.

No sooner had the controversy over this quieted down than another little boy picked up a leather ottoman from among the patio furniture beside the pool and threw it into the water. To his apparent surprise, it promptly sank to the bottom. "I thought it would float," said the moppet as Mrs. Gordon glared at him. "We have one at our house that we put in the pool and it floats."

Lunch was called at one-thirty. The boys and girls, now dried off and back in their party clothes again, sat down at the long, beautifully decorated banquet table (from Abbey Rents, of course) that was set up beside the pool, and put on their paper hats. When there was a slight wait for the hamburgers, which the butler was barbecuing on a brazier a few feet away, the children grew impatient.

"When do we eat?" Tommy Desmond called out.

"Yeah, I'm starved," yelled another.

Then Ronnie Seckler, whose father had once produced a prison picture for Columbia, started banging on his glass with his silverware, and the rest of the children joined in, just the way they do at Sing Sing.

"The eats'll be here in a minute," said Red with a saccharine smile, for he truly loved children, even these. To prove it, he put on a paper hat and made a funny face.

When this failed to quell the incipient riot, he wheeled a spinet piano out from under the patio overhang and announced he would sing a few songs for them while they were waiting. Red can put over a song with the best of them. In fact, a good deal of his fame and fortune came from his ability to sing humorous songs, with very fast, tongue-twisting lyrics.

Red led off with the biggest tongue-twister of all—"When You're Lying Awake," from *Iolanthe*. He was breathless when he finished it.

Somebody applauded—I think it was the butler—and then a little boy said, "I don't like that square stuff. Don't you know any rock and roll?"

Red wasn't a bit annoyed, for he truly understands children. However, he didn't know any rock and roll, and to cover up, he immediately began singing "Dinah," in a Russian dialect, and very rapidly. This didn't seem to go over any better than the first song. Ignoring Red, the children started snapping their snappers and blowing their tin horns. Luckily, Red was saved from any further embarrassment by the arrival of the food.

The conversation at lunch fairly sparkled with racy dialogue. I wasn't able to catch all of it over the noise of the snappers and horns and the rustling of paper hats, but what I was able to hear was quite revealing.

"Did you see Jayne Mansfield in *Rock Hunter?*" one nine-year-old whose name was George asked the boy next to him.

"Not yet, but I want to."

"She sure sticks out in front. Zowie!"

"My dad says they aren't real," interjected a pig-tailed girl from across the table.

"How's he know?"

"He's a producer. He once produced one of her pictures."

"So?" asked George, somewhat belligerently.

"So he's seen her up close."

George regarded her with scorn. "I just hope you stick out as much when you grow up."

"Don't worry," said the little girl confidently.

If the dialogue was somewhat irregular for a children's party, so was the dessert course. In addition to the regulation birthday cake, there was vanilla ice cream smothered in cherries jubilee made with Napoleon brandy. I'm not sure why the Gordons chose to serve this. If they hoped that some of the children would pass out from the effects of the brandy, they had grossly underestimated these children. The cherries jubilee only made them more obstreperous. They immediately started sailing their paper plates out across the swimming pool, emulating flying saucers. Others sailed their plates straight up like earth satellites, while others took pot shots at them with their favors. One boy even threw his glass of milk in the water.

By then even Red was beginning to lose his patience. "Okay, simmer down, everybody," he shouted in a kindly voice. "If you don't start behaving, there'll be no movies."

This admonition deterred nobody. They stopped making flying saucers when they were good and ready, which was when there were no plates or table decorations left that weren't in the swimming pool.

"All right, movietime, everybody," announced Red gaily. "Everyone into the projection room. I've got a big treat for you."

The big treat just happened to be a comedy starring Red Gordon. It was called *The Streetcar Conductor*. It wasn't one

of his more recent films, but, as he explained in an aside to me, it was the only one of his pictures that he owned a print of. "But the kids'll eat it up," he added

Out of respect to the birthday girl's father, there was a minimum of jeering and booing when the title of the picture was flashed on the screen, and then the children quieted their voices to a pitch where you could almost hear the dialogue of the movie.

After the picture had been on about ten minutes, one little girl named Molly Gimble stood up and walked to the door, where Red Gordon was standing laughing at his screen antics.

"Where are you going?" he asked her.

"Out," she replied.

"Why?"

Molly gave him a devastating look. "Mr. Gordon," she said, "this is the fifth birthday party in a row of Judy's that you've shown this same picture. I'm sick, sick, sick of it."

She flounced out the door, and the picture continued.

Ten minutes later one of the boys walked to the door.

"I'm going to the bathroom," he explained to Red. "And don't save my seat!"

Thereafter, at shorter and shorter intervals, the rest of the children deserted the projection room, one by one, and didn't return.

By the end of the second reel, the only persons remaining were the Gordons and I. Even Judy, the birthday girl, had disappeared.

Personally, I thought the picture was quite funny, so I stuck it out with the Gordons until the very end. At this point we heard the sound of much laughter, and a little girl's piercing cry, coming from the living room.

We rushed in to see what it was all about, and we found the children seated on the terrazzo floor in a large circle. In the center of the circle was an empty Scotch bottle on its side. Nearby, two of the boys were holding Molly pinned to the floor, while a third one, Ronnie Seckler, was trying to kiss her on the lips.

"What's this all about?" asked Mrs. Gordon.

"We were playing spin-the-bottle," explained Judy, with an impish laugh. "And Molly doesn't want to let Ronnie kiss her."

87

"Then she shouldn't have to," said Mrs. Gordon, as the boys released Molly. "And Ronnie, you should know better than to try to force her. That's not very gentlemanly."

"Aw, she's a prude," said Ronnie. "I'm never going to invite her to one of my parties."

"Well, I think that's quite enough spin-the-bottle for one day," said Mrs. Gordon, confiscating the bottle. "You children better start behaving like little ladies and gentlemen, or I'm going to send you all home."

The children repaired to the pool for the rest of the afternoon. There, when they weren't actually swimming and trying to drown one another, they amused themselves by filling balloons with water and dropping "bombs" on the roof of the house next door, which was on a lower level.

The Gordons made a perfunctory effort to stop them, but when they realized it couldn't be done they decided to ignore the children's capers, and they invited me to join them in the barroom for what they wearily referred to as a "daycap."

While we were blissfully ignoring the balloon-throwing orgy, the doorbell rang, and a uniformed gentleman from the Beverly Hills police force presented himself, carrying the limp remains of some broken, wet balloons.

Beverly Hills policemen have a reputation for being extremely polite, especially in their dealings with A Group homeowners. And this one was no exception. He refrained from saying, "This is a raid," although, in actuality, it was. He merely informed the Gordons that the people next door had phoned in a complaint, and he warned them that the balloon-dropping bit had better stop.

The party never quite got going again after the sobering effect of the policeman's visit. The children's spirits seemed to be crushed.

Nevertheless, I thought that the group as a whole showed considerable promise that afternoon. Just give them a few years to develop, and get them all together again, and I predict there will be a wild party in Hollywood yet.

And I hope they don't forget to invite me.

7

Do Not Covet Thy Neighbor's Life

"Boy, you sure have an ideal life," a friend said to me one day. "Every morning I have to drive fifteen miles to my office downtown. All you have to do when you get up in the morning is step into the next room, and you're at work."

He's right about one thing—stepping into the next room. But whether I'm at work or not is a moot question. Certainly nobody *thinks* I am.

For several years now, the same employee of the United Parcel Service has been delivering packages to our house. If no one else is home, which is often the case, I have to go to the door when he rings and accept the package myself. Until recently, it's been a very impersonal relationship. He handed me the package without saying a word, and I slammed the door in his face and scurried back to my typewriter. But the last time he handed me a package, he looked at me curiously for a moment, and then said, "Mr. Marx, I sure feel sorry for your wife."

"How's that?" I said.

"Well, what I mean is—don't you think it's about time you went to work?"

The neighbors are fully convinced I'm a bum, too. They don't actually come out and say so, but their behavior speaks for itself. They feel free to drop in on me and gossip and have a free cup of coffee whenever the mood strikes them. If they don't come personally, they'll send their children over to play at our house. They know that if Irene isn't home that someone—good old reliable Steve and Andy's daddy—will always be around to act as playground director. He won't mind taking time out from whatever it is he's doing to phone the emergency hospital when one of the kids falls out of a tree, or to referee the numerous backyard brawls that take place outside his study window.

The children—theirs and mine—hold me in the same high regard as the grownups do.

"My daddy goes to an office," I heard the neighbor's boy telling Andy outside my study window. "Why doesn't your daddy do something?"

"I just don't know," said Andy.

That night Andy said to me, "Why don't you go to an office and do something like George's father does?"

I'm sure it never occurred to either of these upstarts that George's father may not be doing anything more important in his office than chasing his secretary around the desk. It may have occurred to George's mother, but she hasn't confided in me.

Anyway, the point is I'm not getting the kind of respect that is good for one's morale. I'm not getting the kind of lunches that are good for one's morale, either.

In the business world, lunchtime is a pleasant interlude in the day. But not in my world. While other men are out at noon cultivating business contacts, sipping martinis and devouring sumptuous businessmen's luncheons at Romanoff's or The Brown Derby (and writing it all off their income taxes), what am I doing? I'm home in our kitchen, nibbling on last week's leftovers —usually the ones that won't go down the garbage disposal: cold oxtails, or perhaps an old roast-reef bone that our dog has graciously consented to let me gnaw on first.

Aside from the humiliation I suffer daily, there is a more practical aspect of my work to consider: getting some pages written. This, I like to believe, is the main object of this peculiar existence I lead. But with all the things I have to do around the house during the day, my writing is actually pretty much of a sideline.

Screaming at the children to be quiet ("Don't you know Daddy's trying to work?") or to go to somebody else's house and play ("Why don't you go to George's? Nobody's trying to work there.") is one of my most time-consuming diversions. I have to do this approximately every five minutes. Steve and Andy have high-pitched voices that carry about two hundred yards when they aren't even trying. They also have a fairly impressive arsenal of toy guns that make such a racket that the children can't even hear me yelling at them. Not that it would help any if they could, for they just don't seem to understand *why* I want them to be quiet, and I don't think they ever will.

I once gave Andy a long and severe lecture on the importance of not disturbing me and keeping his voice down to a small roar while I was trying to work.

"Sure, I know what you mean, Daddy," he said when I was finished.

But about an hour later he came tiptoeing into my study and over to my desk.

"Can I talk to you?" he whispered loudly in my ear.

"I thought I told you not to bother me when I'm working."

"I'm not bothering you now, Daddy. I'm whispering. Isn't that being quiet enough?"

When Irene is home, she acts as the buffer state between me and the children. *She* screams at them to be quiet. The only trouble with this arrangement is that I have to yell at Irene to be quiet.

However, screaming at the children only takes up about half of my working day. The other half is devoted to—well, to practically everything but writing.

Any household crisis—and there are thirty or forty of them on a good day—is the signal to consult Daddy.

In addition to working on appliances and serving subpoenas, I am available for getting rid of ants, picking up our laundress at the bus station, moving furniture, helping Irene out with the PTA tea and any number of other sundry and uninspiring chores.

That's where the office worker has it all over me. If I were a gray-flannel-suit-type fellow, Irene wouldn't dream of asking me to leave my office to investigate the presence of ants in the powder room, or to ride down to school with her so I could carry the "heavy samovar" for the PTA tea. The PTA would get along with tea bags, and Andy would still wind up with a "C" in arithmetic.

But since Daddy is only working in the next room (and not really working but sleeping, everyone assumes), what is the harm in getting him to help out for a few minutes? The break will probably do him good. At least it will wake him up.

Conversely, things are really no better when I'm home alone—Irene being at the market, and both children off at school. "You'll be able to get lots of pages written while I'm gone," Irene confidently assures me before leaving the house. "There won't be a single soul to disturb you."

But this will be the day that every tradesman in town picks to turn up at our house to perform his particular service: the laundry man (Irene forgot to strip the beds, and I have to do that for her); the Fuller Brush man; one of our stable of appliance repairmen; the County Tax Assessor (I have to think of all kinds of lies to tell him); the exterminator, who insists that I clear out of the house for at least an hour while he lays down a cloud of deadly insecticide spray; and, of course, the United Parcel man, with *his* slurring remarks.

"I don't think you should go out any more," I complained to Irene one morning as she was about to embark on a shopping expedition. "Every time I'm here alone I spend the entire day answering the door."

"Well, I can't not grocery shop," she said. "We'd all starve to death."

"We will anyway, if I don't finish this article I was supposed to have in New York last Wednesday."

"I have a very simple suggestion," said Irene. "Don't answer the doorbell if it rings. Let whoever it is come back some other time—when I'm here."

A sound idea, on the face of it.

I had been working possibly for ten minutes when I heard the doorbell ring the first time. I laughed, pretending it was the bell on my typewriter, and kept right on working.

The bell ringer was a little more persistent the second time he rang. He kept his finger on the button for about seven minutes, at the same time kicking at the new paint job on the back door with what must have been mountain-climbing boots. I couldn't exactly ignore this racket, but neither was I going to give in and answer the door.

And I didn't have to. The bell ringer soon quit the back door, walked into our yard and over to the window of my study.

"Kaufman, the Cleaner!" he called out cheerfully, holding a pair of my flannel slacks on a hanger up to the window.

What was I supposed to do—tell him to go away and take the chance of his leaving my good slacks outside for the dog to rip to pieces? And as long as I had to interrupt my work to accept the slacks, I might just as well hunt around for some of the other garments we wanted to send out to be cleaned.

The rest of the tradesmen who dropped in that morning found me without any difficulty, either. There was the usual assortment, plus a very insistent, horse-faced lady who insisted that no family should be without *The Book of Knowledge*.

"Nobody in this family can READ!" I finally had to say, slamming the door in her face.

As I returned to my study, I was grateful for one thing—I wouldn't be bothered again. I couldn't be. There was nobody left in town who hadn't already been to see me.

About fifteen minutes later, I was breezing along at the typewriter—so absorbed in my work I didn't even hear the doorbell ring. When I finally looked up, I saw Betty Sharp, the attractive young housewife who lives next door, standing outside my window.

I glared at her, real friendly-like, and continued to type.

"Could you please stop whatever it is you're doing for a minute?" she said, pressing her nose against the window pane. "I'm in terrible trouble!"

Even Arnold Bennett, with his schedule of five thousand words before breakfast, couldn't have resisted the distress call of such a lovely neighbor.

"What's the matter?" I asked, meeting her at the back door.

"The darnedest thing just happened," she explained breathlessly. "I went to get in my car to go downtown, and then I discovered I left my car keys in the house. And my house key, too. And the emergency door key Harry and I keep under the mat just won't turn the lock. I think the lock is stuck. I wonder if you would try turning it for me? You're so much stronger than I am."

I spent the next hour wrestling with the lock on her front door. When all my attempts to work the jammed lock failed, Betty said, "Do you mind if I use your phone to call Harry at the office? He'll have to come home and let me in."

Of course I didn't mind. But Charlie did. He was in a very important conference and wouldn't even talk with his wife.

"I guess I'll just have to wait and call him again in a few minutes," said Betty, sitting down on the couch with a sigh, and lighting a cigarette. "Do you mind?"

"Delighted to help out," I said, never feeling less delighted in my life.

"You wouldn't happen to have a spare cup of coffee around, would you?" asked Betty.

"No, but I suppose I could make some."

"Oh, I wouldn't want to put you to any bother."

After I made a pot of coffee, and we were on our second cup, she tried Harry again. But he still refused to talk.

"I don't know what I'm going to do," said Betty anxiously. "I have to be downtown at a Ladies Auxiliary meeting in thirty minutes. And I have to introduce the guest speaker."

It would have been pretty mean of me to leave the guest speaker standing unintroduced on the podium all day. After all, he might be an old man, and maybe he'd have a heart attack from standing too long. However, since I didn't feel I could spare the time to drive Betty downtown (although she had made several hints to the effect that I might enjoy the lecture), I volunteered to climb up on the Sharps' roof and try to gain entrance through a second-story window that appeared to be open.

94

I managed to reach the window, after scrounging around the neighborhood for a long-enough ladder and a Dramamine tablet to keep me from getting airsick. But it only appeared to be open. It wasn't really.

"Then would you mind trying the door that goes out to that up-stairs sun porch?" Betty called out. "Sometimes we leave that open."

I made my way across the slippery red tile roof, and climbed over the railing to the porch, tearing my pants in the bargain. The door wasn't open, but the lock seemed to be flimsy enough to break.

"I could probably pry it open if I had some tools," I yelled down.

"Would you hurry?" she called out. "I really have to get going."

I climbed down the ladder, procured a screwdriver and pliers from our garage, and clambered back up to the porch again. I had just broken the lock when the telephone rang inside the Sharps' bedroom.

"Hurry up and answer it," Betty Sharp exhorted me. "It may be something important."

I hurried, ripping my coat pocket on the doorknob as I went into the house, and reached the phone just in time. It was Harry Sharp, returning his wife's call.

"What the hell are *you* doing in my house?" he said suspiciously, after I told him who I was.

I had a tough time assuring Charlie that I was not a rival for his wife's affections, but after I explained the circumstances in great detail he seemed to understand. In fact, he said, rather gratefully, "Well, it's a damn lucky thing you hang around the house all day. Otherwise I would have blown a big deal having to stop what I was doing to get my scatterbrained wife back into the house."

As I was leaving the Sharps' house via the front door, Irene drove up into our driveway with a carful of groceries and noticed me standing there talking with Betty.

"I thought you were working this morning," Irene called over.

95

"I've been helping Betty out," I said.

"Nice work if you can get it," Irene said, in what could be interpreted as a skeptical tone.

"Your husband's been such a doll," said Betty. "I got locked out and he helped me get back in. I really put him to a lot of bother, but I don't know what I would have done without him."

"Well, as long as you're being so gallant today," Irene said to me, "how about coming over to your *own* house and helping me carry the groceries in?"

8

Grandpa Groucho and Marilyn Monroe

My son Steve has a number of good qualities, but neatness has never been one of them. I suppose this is because, like most eight-year-old boys, he's a born collector. I mean, there's no telling what you're liable to find among the assorted toys and litter in his bedroom. It could be anything from a dead salamander in a tin can to a pair of 1946 Mississippi license plates.

Consequently, Irene and I are rarely surprised by the things we do find in Steve's bedroom.

I could say "never," but that wouldn't be quite true. Once we *were* surprised when we came across one of Steve's collector's items—extremely so. It happened one summer evening when we were putting him and Andy to bed.

While the children were getting into their pajamas, I saw, sticking out from under a comic book on Steve's desk, an interesting work of art. It was a glossy 3 x 3 snapshot of Marilyn Monroe in the nude—the handy wallet-size reproduction of her world-famous calendar picture.

"Say, where'd you get this?" I asked Steve, holding up the picture and whistling wolfishly.

Steve blushed and, after a great deal of hemming and hawing, finally said, not too convincingly, "I found it on a vacant lot."

Irene and I exchanged looks of disbelief, and then I noticed that the picture had been torn in half and put back together again with Scotch tape.

"How did it get ripped?" I asked Steve.

"Andy tried to take it away from me," he replied, glaring down at his little brother.

"It looks as if we have a Marilyn Monroe fan club springing up in our midst," said Irene, slightly alarmed.

After a brief conference, Irene and I decided to let Steve keep the photo he had found. After all, he was eight years old now, and we didn't want him to think there was anything wrong with showing what we felt was a normal and healthy curiosity about sex.

Of course, we still weren't completely convinced that he had found the picture on a vacant lot. You just don't find nude pictures of Marilyn Monroe on vacant lots—at least not in *our* neighborhood (at least *I* never have).

But since we had no evidence to refute his statement, and since a man is presumed to be innocent until he's proven guilty—even in our house—we decided to drop the subject.

A few days later the four of us were attending a birthday party that my father was throwing for his daughter, Melinda (my baby sister), at Blum's Ice Cream Parlor in Beverly Hills. While we were eating our ice cream and cake, Marilyn Monroe's name happened to come up in the conversation—probably because Father was taking the group of seven- and eight-year-olds to see *The Seven Year Itch* immediately following the festivities.

Naturally, this reminded me of Steve's Marilyn Monroe photograph, and, thinking my father might be amused, I related to him the incident of finding the snapshot on his grandson's desk.

Father was amused, but not as amused as he was concerned.

"Very interesting," he said, looking extremely serious under his paper party hat. "Are you sure he found it on a vacant lot?"

"That's what he told me. Why?"

"Well"—Father seemed reluctant to say this—"I haven't seen *my* picture of Marilyn Monroe around lately."

"Do you have one, too?" I asked, surprised.

"I *had* one." His voice was filled with disgust. "I used to keep it on my desk—for a gag, of course," he added hastily.

"Do you suppose—?"

"I don't know," he said anxiously. "I'll look for it as soon as I get home."

The next time I saw my father—at his house—he confirmed his suspicions. "It's gone," he said glumly. "I can't find my picture of Marilyn anywhere!"

This revelation, combined with the fact that Steve had spent the weekend at his grandfather's house several weeks prior to his finding the picture on "a vacant lot," added up to a fairly convincing piece of circumstantial evidence.

Irene and I could hardly wait to return home to confront Steve with it. When we did, he broke down almost immediately and confessed to taking the picture from his grandfather when he had spent the weekend at his house.

His motive: he had heard several of his boy friends in the neighborhood discussing the severe shortage of Marilyn Monroe "nudes," and he, in order to show them what a big man he was, had said he knew where he could get one. (Evidently, he'd had his eye on it for some time.)

Irene and I promptly sat Steve down, and gave him a long, stern, and I'm sure dull, lecture on stealing. And we concluded by telling him that he'd have to return the picture to his grandfather and make an apology the next time the family got together, which was to be the following evening, when we were all going downtown to see a production of *Pinafore* at the Biltmore Theater.

Steve said he didn't mind having to give up the picture (although he preferred not to), but he asked if it would be all right to apologize to my father in writing. He said he was too ashamed to confess to the crime in person.

We told him we supposed it would be all right, and he went straight to his desk and wrote the following note:

> DEAR GRANDPA GROUCHO,
> I am very sorry I took your picture of Marilyn Monroe. I will not do it again.
>
> > Love,
> > STEVE

He put the note in an envelope, and with it he enclosed the Marilyn Monroe snapshot and a one-dollar bill. He didn't explain what the money was for, and we didn't ask him, but I presumed it was for "damages."

The next evening, when we were picking my father up at his house, Steve handed him the note of apology and asked him to open it in private. Father promised, but during the long ride downtown he couldn't contain his curiosity. When Steve was gazing out the window, Father sneaked a look at the letter, and then, with an amused smile, slipped the picture and the dollar bill back into his coat pocket.

Irene and I noticed him doing this, and we figured that sometime before the end of the evening Father would undoubtedly take Steve aside, give him a kindly talking to about the evils of stealing, forgive him officially, and return the dollar to him. After all, what did a man in Father's tax bracket need with Steve's dollar?

But as the evening progressed, nothing like that happened. The dollar remained securely in Father's pocket throughout the entire two acts of *Pinafore*, and also while we were having a soda after the show. It looked very much as if Father meant to keep the dollar for good. The affair of the Marilyn Monroe picture was now a closed book to him.

When we were walking to the parking lot, Irene nudged me hard in the ribs and whispered in an annoyed tone, "Don't tell me your father's going to *keep* Steve's dollar?"

"I don't know," I shrugged. "Maybe he wants to teach him a lesson."

"Well, if he does that to Steve after Steve was good enough to give him all the money he's been saving up, I'll never speak to him again," threatened Irene, glaring at the back of Father's head.

"Steve gave it to him," I said, trying to keep a vendetta from getting started. "Father probably doesn't want to hurt his feelings by giving it back."

"I don't care—I never heard of such a mean thing," said Irene.

"Why—do you know how much a dollar is? It's ten weeks' allowance."

"Forget it," I said. "I'll give him a dollar myself."

But Irene couldn't forget it. On the way home in the car, she flatly refused to speak to my father (which, fortunately, for the good of the evening, he didn't even notice because he was so busy talking himself), and I have to admit I was getting slightly annoyed at him, too.

About the only one in our family who wasn't at all upset over the loss of the dollar was Steve. He accepted it as a matter of course that Grandpa Groucho would keep the money, and while we were driving home he and Melinda chatted happily in the back seat.

At midnight, I parked the car in front of my father's house, and everybody alighted. While we were saying our assorted thank yous and good-bys, Irene again nudged me in the ribs and said, "Well, you can kiss that *dollar* good-by, too."

And I was inclined to agree with her. But Father double-crossed us both.

Just before he opened his front door, he took me aside and slipped the dollar bill into my hand, unbeknownst to Steve.

"Here," he said. "Give this back to Steve."

He started to unlock the front door, then turned around again and took something else out of his pocket and handed it to me. It was the picture of Marilyn Monroe. "Steve might as well have the picture, too," he added with a smile, at the same time wiggling his eyebrows. "I'm getting too old for that sort of thing."

9

I Was a Prisoner of Den 7

October 1

Steve is joining the Cub Scouts. He came home from school today and said that now that he is eight years old he has decided to take the plunge. Irene and I are delighted. From what we hear about Cub Scouting, we think it will be just the thing to strengthen his character. His character can stand some strengthening, and Cub Scouting ought to turn the trick. It'll keep him out in the open where men are men, and a good toasted marshmallow can make one forget things like nude calendar girls.

October 15

Walked into the living room today and found Steve cramming for his Cub Scout entrance requirements. Irene was helping him memorize the Cub Scout Promise. Later, they ran through the secret signals—Secret Code, Secret Handshake, and the Living Circle. I'm not so sure I approve of all this secret stuff. It teaches boys to be secretive and sneaky, which is just what we're trying to avoid. As I told Irene, next thing you know Steve will be hiding his report card in a pumpkin shell.

October 22

Tonight, at the monthly Pack meeting, in the auditorium of Canyon Elementary School, Steve became a full-fledged Cub Scout.

The oath-taking ceremony was very impressive. Steve and the seven other midgets who are forming the new den stood up in front of the whole Pack and took the oath, thereby becoming Bobcats, the lowest form of Cub Scout life. After that came the moment we'd all been waiting for—the pinning of the Bobcat pins on the new Cubs by their parents. We are still waiting, for the Cub Master had forgotten to order the pins from Cub Scout headquarters.

Afterward, the Cub Master, who looks like Steve Allen but who isn't as amusing (at least not intentionally), explained how "Cubbing," as he referred to it, works. After completing certain achievements, a Bobcat becomes a Wolf. Then he can start working toward his Gold and Silver Arrows, emblematic of more achievements. It is up to the individual parents to test and pass the Cubs on their achievements.

When we were alone, Irene and I both remarked that we hoped Steve's interest in Cubbing wouldn't fizzle out. The discipline and competition should be a marvelous character builder. (How the topic of conversation when we are alone has changed since we were married.)

October 23

Awakened early (5 A.M.) by sounds highly reminiscent of a bowling tournament in living room. I investigated and found Steve practicing tumbling. He explained that he was working on Achievement One for his Wolf Badge—Feats of Skill—and asked if I'd care to see him do a Forward Roll. Before I could say no, he had not only done a Forward and Backward Roll, but he had also climbed to the top of one of our floor lamps to demonstrate his tree-climbing ability. Then he tossed me a baseball mitt and suggested that we have a catch. Being able to throw and catch a ball is part of Feats of Skill.

I told him it was too early for Cubbing. "Oh, guy!" he whined, stomping his foot and petulantly tossing the baseball over his shoulder. To keep the old horsehide from going through our picture window, I made a diving catch of his throw that would have made Willie Mays envious, and then I tossed the ball back to him. "Thanks for having a catch with me, Dad," he said, gloving the ball neatly. "Now you can pass me."

I passed him on his first achievement, but I'm still not certain I approve of any organization that encourages a boy to make a fool of his father.

October 28

Tonight after dinner Steve tried on his Cub Scout uniform for the first time. We discovered that the emblems, which Irene had spent three days attaching to his uniform, weren't sewn on in quite the right places. "Pack Six," for example, was on the left elbow instead of the right shoulder, and "Cub Scouts B.S.A." turned out to be underneath the pocket flap, although Irene insists that when she sewed it on at 3 A.M. Tuesday it was above the pocket flap. Now Irene will have to stay up all night again tonight, sewing, so Steve can wear his uniform to the Den Meeting tomorrow. As a result, she will probably miss seeing the late, late movie on T.V. Too bad. They are playing *Hell's Angels*.

October 29

Steve attended his first Den Meeting today. When he arrived home, his cheeks were a healthy, apple-red color—the color they can only get from being out in the woods on a brisk fall day. "Been hiking?" I asked him. "No, bowling," he replied. "Bowling! What kind of scouting is that?" I exclaimed. "Next week I suppose your Den Mother will be taking you to a pool hall." Steve looked at me critically, and said, "No, not next week, Daddy. The week after. Next week we're going to play miniature golf."

November 19

Steve has been working diligently for the past twenty days in order to complete his first twelve achievements and thus be eligible to receive his Wolf Badge at the monthly meeting of the Pack next week, and he has passed all the requirements. Among other things, he has had to learn how to whittle, make a collection of some kind (other than trying to get his allowance), make a scrap-book, and practice the rules of safety, such as not leaving his roller skates at the top of the stairs. Since there are no stairs in a bungalow, this one had us all baffled for quite some time, but we finally figured out that another rule of safety would also be ac-ceptable, so we substituted not reading in bed by candlelight (a practice he had become addicted to after we had confiscated his flashlight for trying to read after "lights out").

Incidentally, we haven't heard yet whether any of the other boys in the Den will be eligible for their Wolf Badges, but Irene and I hope Steve isn't the only one, as we wouldn't want it to look as if we're pushing him too fast.

November 21

Trouble. Steve came home from school today in tears. He learned that Jeffrey Boswell, one of the Cubs in Den 7, is going to get his Wolf Badge at Friday night's Pack Meeting and a Gold Arrow and two Silver Arrows as well. This means that Jeffrey completed a total of 42 achievements and electives. "He *must* have cheated!" exclaimed Irene, and she called up Jeff's mother to investigate. Mrs. Boswell defended the integrity of her little monster, but finally admitted that Jeffrey had piled up most of his points in the "Helping Around the House" elective, by empty-ing wastebaskets. She gave him one point every time he emptied a wastebasket. "A pretty cheap way to get maid service," I told Irene. She wasn't amused, so I said, "Then why don't you call up the Den Mother and complain about such tactics?" Irene looked scornfully at me and said, "Dear, Mrs. Boswell *is* the Den Mother. And she insists it's perfectly legitimate to award points on that basis."

Seems to me this is a pretty loose interpretation of the rules. It's making a farce out of old Dan Beard. I had to explain to Steve that there's no satisfaction in getting an award you haven't really earned. But Steve's answer to that was, "I don't want any satisfaction. I just want a Gold Arrow."

November 23

Irene spent the day showing Steve how to empty wastebaskets. She says he'll have enough points for a Gold Arrow by bedtime.

November 25

Tonight was Pack Night. Every boy in Den 7 got at least one Gold Arrow. There must be a lot of empty wastebaskets in the neighborhood.

November 29

Steve came back from today's Den Meeting and reported that Mrs. Boswell had taken them bowling again. I called up Mrs. Boswell immediately, and said, "Why don't you let the boys do some handicraft once in a while, instead of taking them bowling all the time?" She said, "As a matter of fact, I have some handicraft planned for next week's Den Meeting—at *your* house."

December 6

I just found out today why the Den Mother has been keeping the Den Meetings away from the homes. The Den Meeting at our house has finally broken up. So has most of the furniture. The furniture that the Cubs weren't able to break is permanently scarred from the wood-burning sets Mrs. Boswell donated to the meeting. We also have Coca-Cola stains on our white ceiling from Coke bottles that have been shaken up and their gaseous contents unleashed. And Andy still hasn't quite recovered from the shock of finding himself lashed to a chair as a result of his wandering through the meeting room just as Mrs. Boswell announced to the Cub Scouts, "Now, let's try our skill at knot tying."

December 15

Hurray! Irene has finally got the hang of being a dishonest Cub Scout mother. Today she and Steve spent the afternoon making Jello, under the Cooking elective. Technically, a Jello-making session is only worth one point, but what Irene did is really ingenious. She had Steve pour the Jello into ten small molds, and is giving him credit for ten batches of Jello. Tomorrow, she tells me, they are going to put Reddi-whip on the ten servings, and that will be good for an additional ten points. At this rate, Steve will be the leader in Silver Arrows at the next Pack Meeting.

December 22

No Pack Meeting this month. It falls too close to Christmas. Well, that's one good thing that can be said of the holiday season, anyway.

January 13

Steve learned today that the other mothers are not only giving one point for each serving of Jello and one point for a glob of Reddi-whip, but they are awarding an additional point for putting fruit in the Jello. I guess Steve will never be top man in the Silver Arrow department. We don't like fruit in our Jello.

February 17

Good news at last. Steve is finally going to get a chance to better himself. Den 7 has been chosen to put on the skit at the March Pack Meeting, and I have been picked to write it. At first I wasn't going to accept the assignment, the pay being what it is, but I changed my mind when Irene pointed out, "If you write and produce the skit, you'll be perfectly justified in giving the leading role to our son." Playing the lead ought to be plenty of compensation to Steve for the fact that he is trailing in the Silver Arrow derby.

March 5

I'm bleary eyed. I had to stay up until four A.M. writing the skit for Pack Night. Originally, I hadn't intended doing it until this weekend, but Mrs. Boswell phoned me after dinner last night and said, "Where's the skit you promised us? We have to start rehearsing it at tomorrow's Den Meeting." I explained that I hadn't got around to writing it yet, as I had a magazine assignment to finish first. But she said, "That's no excuse for a professional writer. You can dash one off in ten minutes, if you'd only knuckle down. Now I expect that skit by tomorrow at the latest, with ten carbons, or else." The "or else" sounded rather ominous, so I decided I'd better do it.

At first I had a little difficulty finding a suitable subject, but I believe I finally came up with a script that really captures the true spirit of Cub Scouting.

The whole skit takes place by the side of a superhighway, where a beautiful eighteen-year-old girl, in a bikini bathing suit, lies beside her bicycle, apparently unconscious. As the curtain rises, some Cub Scouts who've been out on a hike (actually they've been hitching a ride on a truck) enter the scene and notice the lovely creature in distress. "Hey, look at the girl," says the Den Leader. "She must have fallen off her bike and broken her gams." They decide to administer first aid, but they don't have any splints. "Use your ingenuity like a good Cub Scout should," says an eerie offstage voice. This starts the boys thinking in the right direction, so they chop down a tree and cut it up into splints. Just as they are applying the splints to the girl's legs, she awakens and, not knowing what they are up to, she screams for help. A passing motorcycle cop stops and wants to know what's going on. The girl explains that she was trying to take a nap by the side of the road when she was accosted by these strange, blue-suited creatures who, she was pretty sure, had come off a flying saucer. "We're Cub Scouts, ma'am," retorts one of the boys. "And we thought you were injured." "Well, whoever they are, they're awfully fresh!" exclaims the girl. Being an easy mark for a well-turned ankle, the officer is inclined to side with the girl, and is about to run the boys into the station on a delinquency charge when one of the Cubs recognizes the girl for what she is. "You know what, Officer?" he says. "She's the one who ought to be arrested. This is Naughty Nellie, the Sex Bandit. She lies by the side of roads and pretends she's injured, so men like us will stop and help her. And then she robs them! I read all about her in my *True Detective* comic book." Well, the Cub turns out to be right, the girl is arrested, and Den 7 gets the $10,000 reward, which they turn over to charity, except for five dollars which they keep to restock the Den's comic-book library.

March 6

Irene is quite upset because of what happened at yesterday's Den Meeting. After I read the play aloud for the boys and Mrs. Boswell, all of whom were delighted with it, I began assigning the parts. "Steve, you can be the policeman," I said casually. But Steve announced that he didn't want to be the policeman. "Don't you know your daddy wrote that part especially for you?" asked Irene, trying hard not to lose her patience. "I don't care," replied Steve. "I want to play the offstage voice. It's more fun being a spook!"

Irene told him he ought to have more ambition than that, but Steve couldn't be dissuaded, so finally we had to give his part to someone else. Very disappointing. You start out with such high hopes and dreams for your children, and they wind up wanting to be nothing more than offstage voices.

March 18

Irene is feeling better now. I've finagled things around so that Steve will be the one to come out on the stage before the curtain goes up and announce to the audience the name of the skit and give the credits. As I told Irene, this is the kind of acting that really pays off nowadays. Look at Ed Sullivan.

March 31

There is one difference between Steve and Ed Sullivan that didn't occur to me until I was watching Steve's performance at the Pack Meeting last night. Ed Sullivan uses a teleprompter; Steve had to rely on his memory, which is none too reliable. Not only didn't he mention the title of the play, but, more important, he forgot to say who wrote it. Moreover, his offstage voice couldn't be heard in the audience. That's because he was a little too far offstage. He was, in fact, out in the corridor getting a drink of water at the time he was supposed to be saying his one line, and he didn't return until the play was over. Anyway, the rest of the performance was a huge success, and I'm glad I put the skit on for them. It was time-consuming, but at least now I've fulfilled my obligations to the Cub Scouts. No one can say I'm one of those fathers who doesn't pitch in.

May 16

Irene looked across the dinner table at me tonight, and said sweetly, "You look very tired and run-down, dear. What you need is a couple of days off in the country." I swallowed the bait like an unwary salmon. "I guess I could use a brief vacation," I admitted. "Then it's all settled," she said. "What's all settled?" I asked. "That you'll take Steve on the overnight hike on Memorial Day weekend," she replied. I reminded her that she said I needed a rest, and that I didn't think hiking through the underbrush and sleeping on the damp ground with a bunch of snakes, to say nothing of Cub Scouts, came under that category. "Steve will be heartbroken if he doesn't get to go," she said. "He can go. I just don't want to go," I said. "You know very well that each Cub Scout has to be accompanied by his father," said Irene. "And it's only once a year. And all the other fathers are doing it. So why can't you do that much for your son?" That's when I really told her off. I said that I didn't like hiking, that I had done my bit for the Cub Scouts by writing a play for them, and furthermore, if Steve couldn't go on the hike without me, he'd have to stay home. Either that, or Irene could put on slacks and a sweatshirt and go in my place. "After all," I concluded, "I have a life to live, too."

May 25

I just returned from Nelson's Sporting Goods Store, where I spent a small fortune outfitting us with the latest camping equipment: sleeping bags, rubber inflatable mattresses, snake repellent, cooking utensils, pickaxes, rope and flares. I never thought I'd get a kick out of this sort of thing, but now I find

I'm actually looking forward to the hike with Steve. It'll probably do us both good to get away from civilization for a change.

May 27

Bud Wayne phoned and said that he and the rest of the fathers in Den 7 have been talking it over, and that they would rather not go on the hike for various reasons: this is the foggy season and a couple of the boys always get colds when they sleep out of doors; one of the fathers has to attend a party Saturday night and can't miss it for business reasons; and another one of the fathers owns a delicatessen in Santa Monica and this is his weekend to be the maître de. In addition, the fathers feel it is wasteful to spend a lot of money on camping equipment just to be gone one night. So the overnight hike is off. Instead, Bud and I and a couple of the other fathers are going to take the boys on an official "cook-out" in Tapia Park during the day on Memorial Day. According to Bud Wayne, the Cubs will enjoy that just as much. Maybe more, because they'll be home in time to see *Lassie* on T.V.

May 28

Spent the afternoon trying to get Nelson's Sporting Goods to take back the camping equipment, but Nelson refused. At first he said it was his policy never to take back merchandise, but when I became insistent, he pretended he had never seen me before and said I must have bought the equipment elsewhere. Irene says it serves me right for not believing in charge accounts, and for paying cash for goods.

May 29

Bud Wayne phoned again, and the plan is this: he will pick me and Steve up in his station wagon early tomorrow morning. He'll take half the group with him, and half will go with Herb Baker in his station wagon. We'll bring raw steaks, and we'll barbecue them at Tapia Park, where they have barbecue pits and grates for the campers. I'm hungry just thinking about those steaks sizzling over an open fire.

May 30

The cook-out began promisingly enough, although we didn't get off to quite the early start we had anticipated. Bud overslept and didn't come by for us until eleven-thirty. I overslept, too; otherwise I would have phoned him and told him to hurry. Anyway, we proceeded by the most direct route to Tapia Park. But traffic was heavy—we'd forgotten about it being Memorial Day —and by the time Den 7 arrived there, the park was so overcrowded that we couldn't get a barbecue pit. In fact, we couldn't even find a place to park our cars. Being Cub Scouts, we naturally had to keep a stiff upper lip, and do the next best thing. We drove along the beach on Highway 101, looking for another spot where we could build a fire. But everywhere it was the same —burning wasn't permitted. If only we had brought sandwiches instead of raw steaks, we could have sat in the station wagons and eaten our lunch. If we could have found a place to park along the highway, that is. But as I say, it was Memorial Day, and quite a few other people had the same idea. There wasn't a single parking space between Santa Barbara and San Diego. We had to keep mushing on. By two o'clock the children were beginning to whine that they were hungry, and by three o'clock they were threatening to mutiny if they didn't get something to eat pretty soon. By four o'clock we were thinking of drawing straws and eating the loser. It was at that point that Billy Singer showed what kind of a Cub Scout he is. He said, "My daddy owns a delicatessen in Santa Monica. Why don't we go *there* and have lunch?" It was the grossest insult that could possibly have been given to a group of Cub Scouts on an official cook-out. And coming from a boy who was allegedly a Cub himself, it bordered on the blasphemous. Nevertheless, we jumped at the opportunity to dine at Singer's Delicatessen, for a corned-beef sandwich on rye with a side of dill pickles is not to be sneezed at when you haven't had anything to eat in over six hours.

June 3

That's the last cook-out I go on. I guess I'm not the type to rough it. For three days, I have had indigestion from eating a dill pickle that was too raw. Moreover, I just received a bill from Singer for my share of the table leg Steve and his fellow Cubs mutilated with their little Scout hatchets while they were waiting for their peanut-butter-and-jelly sandwiches.

June 4

I've definitely made up my mind. I'm going to suggest to Irene that we let Steve resign from the Cub Scouts at the end of the school semester. I don't think it's doing him any good (and I know it's not doing me any good). This morning's incident was the clincher. While I was hunting for my roll of Scotch tape in Steve's desk, I came across his Cub Scout scrapbook—the one he made for Achievement 7. On page one was the nude of Marilyn Monroe. The rest of the book consists of clippings from *Confidential* magazine.

June 5

Steve absolutely refuses to quit the Cub Scouts—he claims he's having too good a time. Besides, he wants to become a Bear, a Lion and then a Webelo. This will take another three years and about twelve hundred dollars' worth of Jello. I wish I'd never been born.

10

The Lucky Bag

Of all the disciplinary problems Irene and I have had to solve, what makes us the proudest is how we finally taught Steve and Andy to keep their rooms neat and their toys and other belongings in order.

For many months, this one was a real challenge to us. Steve and Andy just had no sense of responsibility about their possessions. They would leave their toys on the floor or wherever they happened to be when they were finished playing with them. It seemed to be against their rules of fair play to put anything back on a shelf or in a drawer. At the end of the day, Irene and I would have to spend a couple of hours cleaning up after them.

And it didn't do a bit of good to scold the children about their untidy habits, or to point out to them that the simplest method of keeping their rooms neat was to play with one toy at a time, and put it back on the shelf before selecting another one. "Yes, Mommy," or "Yes, Daddy," they'd answer as they took another armful of toys off the shelf and dumped them on the floor. But that evening we'd again have to spend a lot of time putting their toys away for them.

"We'll just have to do something to teach them to be neat!" Irene said to me one evening when she was down on her hands and knees in Andy's room, hunting under the bed for the top of the Lincoln Log box. "I can't go through this routine the rest of my life."

"I have an idea," I said. "Why don't we put the Lucky Bag system into effect?"

"What on earth is that?" asked Irene.

I explained to her that when I was in the Coast Guard, the sergeant-at-arms of our barracks had what he referred to as a "Lucky Bag" in the bosun's locker. Whenever he found any of our belongings lying around on our bunks or on the deck, he would impound them and put them in the Lucky Bag, and there they would remain until the end of the month, when they would be redeemable on request.

"That's a marvelous idea!" exclaimed Irene. "You're a genius."

Before we tucked Steve and Andy into their beds that evening, we explained to them how the Lucky Bag system worked.

"From now on," Irene warned them, "any toys we find that haven't been put away in their proper places will be picked up and put in the Lucky Bag. Mommy's closet will be the Lucky Bag."

"And you won't get them back until the end of the month, either," I added sternly. "Is that clear?"

"Yes, Daddy. Yes, Mommy."

I'll admit that the first few days of the new regime were pretty hard on the children. They couldn't seem to get it through their little heads that if they left a toy around untended, it was going to be gobbled up by the big bad Lucky Bag.

I'll never forget the first time Andy made the discovery that something of his was missing. "I can't find my bike," he came crying to us. "There must be robbers in Pacific Palisades."

"There aren't any robbers, dear," explained Irene patiently. "You left your bike on the front steps, so I had to put it in the Lucky Bag." (Fortunately for Irene, whose closet isn't too spacious, it was only a sixteen-inch bike.)

"Oh, guy!" exclaimed Andy, bursting into tears.

Steve was extremely shocked and surprised, too, when he discovered that his football was in the Lucky Bag. After he threatened to run away from home, I began to wonder if the Lucky Bag system was too harsh on the children. But Irene convinced me that it was teaching them a much-needed lesson.

There was one slight drawback. Steve and Andy weren't learning the lesson as quickly as we would have liked them to, considering the size of our closets.

By the end of two weeks, Irene's closet was filled to capacity, and I was getting the overflow, which consisted of Steve's entire electric train setup, complete with tunnels, station and power pack, Andy's punching bag, Steve's erector set, nine Hardy Boys mystery books, and a live frog in a glass jar.

By the end of two and a half weeks, my closet was full and so was the guest closet in the front hall. We were running out of places to use for a Lucky Bag.

"I know it hasn't been a month yet," I suggested to Irene one night, "but now that the kids have got the idea, why don't we let them have all their toys back now and they can start over with a clean slate?"

"Good idea," Irene agreed. "I can't wait to get my closet cleaned out. I've been looking for my red shoes for a whole week, but I can't seem to find them under that pile of toys."

Knowing they'd be delirious with joy, we summoned the children, kissed them warmly and told them they could have their toys back.

"But it's only been two and a half weeks," Steve protested. "We don't really deserve to—"

"I know how long it's been," I said, admiring his integrity. "But your mother and I are letting you kids off the hook early this time because we feel sorry for you. But next time we're going to make you stick it out for the whole month, so be careful. Now go on and take your toys back."

A pained expression crossed Steve's face as he said, "I'd just as soon wait, if you don't mind, Daddy. My room's kind of crowded now."

"Crowded? With what?"

"My rock collection. I've got my rocks spread out all over the shelves."

Obviously, it would have been very bad strategy to *make* them take their toys back against their wills at this point, but we were determined not to let them get away with any such nonsense at the end of the month. The toys belonged to them, and they would just have to take them off our hands when the time came, rock collection or not.

Meanwhile, we took great pains to stay out of their rooms, for fear we might find more fodder for the Lucky Bag. And when we did have to trespass in their quarters for some reason, we made certain not to notice the many toys, to say nothing of the small boulders belonging to Steve's rock collection, that were strewn around the room.

However, it wasn't always easy to overlook their slovenly habits —not with the children being as genuinely co-operative about the Lucky Bag as Steve and Andy were. One evening, for instance, I tripped over a toy truck in the front hall. I had no choice but to ignore it as I picked myself up from the floor and headed for the first-aid kit in our bathroom. But Andy chased me to the end of the hall, shoved the truck into my hands, and said, "Here, Daddy— you forgot to put this in the Lucky Bag."

"I didn't forget it," I said. "There just isn't any more room in my closet. As it is, I have to keep two of my suits hanging up in the bathroom—on the shower-curtain pole."

"You could keep your suits in my closet," suggested Steve. "There's plenty of room in there now that there aren't so many toys."

"That's a good idea," said Irene. "Do you mind if I put a few of my dresses in there, too?"

It was inconvenient, of course, having to walk clear down the hall to Steve's room every time I needed a suit or Irene needed a dress. But it was worth it, for it enabled us to follow through with the punishment we'd meted out, thereby demonstrating to the children once again what firm disciplinarians their parents are.

11

A Little Little League Is Too Much

It's an old axiom in sports that "they never come back." Well, it's true, and I can prove it. I coached a little-league baseball team this year, and I'm not coming back next season. This year was quite enough.

I'm still not sure what prompted me to raise my hand when the director of the Sloping Ravine Playground asked for volunteers the night all the parents in our neighborhood met in the playground gym to organize the Little Coast League. I could have sat there with my hands in my pockets, as most of the other fathers were doing, and pretended that unusually heavy business commitments were going to keep me tied up for the entire baseball season.

I could have, but no one would have believed me. The other parents all knew that I was a free-lance writer who worked at home. And since in their eyes this is just one step removed from being a complete bum, it naturally figured that it would be no hardship for *me* to get away from my desk every day to work with the team.

Then, too, there was my friendship with George Brown to consider. George was the father of Steve's best friend, Eddie Brown. We had come to the meeting together, with an eye to getting our two sons on the same team. We felt that this would eliminate the danger of their becoming rivals and possibly winding up bad friends.

George volunteered to manage one of the four teams in our

league, and he chose Eddie and Steve to be on his squad. So when he said he needed a coach to help him—and looked directly at me—I had no choice but to volunteer my services. I couldn't stand by and let George do all the work himself.

Besides, I figured it was important to cement my friendship with the Browns before another day passed. It was important because they had just put a swimming pool in their back yard, and, after all, the hot months were still ahead of us.

Actually, as I found out at the next meeting, which was restricted to managers and coaches, the whole idea of letting the kids get together and play ball was just a way of promoting neighborly friendship among all of us—parents as well as children.

"Remember," said Roy Harris, our muscular playground director, when he was making the keynote speech, "the important thing isn't winning, but letting all the kids participate and have some fun. There's too much emphasis on winning ball games in other little-league setups. Well, we're going to *de*-emphasize winning and concentrate on having a good time."

This gem of a speech got the kind of applause from the rest of the fathers it so richly deserved. It was gratifying to see that we were all in agreement on basic policy.

"And now," continued Harris, "I've got a little surprise for you. I was fortunate to get over here this evening three ex-big leaguers who work for the L.A. Playground Department. They're going to give you some pointers on how to run your teams properly."

He forthwith produced three strapping fellows in sweatshirts and baseball caps who came trotting out of the back room of the gym with baseball bats, gloves, catchers' masks and a large blackboard on tripod legs.

"We gotta lot of ground to cover," said the ballplayer who'd been introduced as Lefty, drawing a baseball diamond on the blackboard. "The sooner you learn the fine points of the game, the sooner you'll be able to start drumming it into the kids' heads, so they won't be making a lot of bonehead plays when the season opens. Now the first thing we'll take up is the Squeeze Play."

121

At this point, Roy Harris interjected with "I hope you coaches and managers brought notebooks and pencils, so you can take notes."

Everyone seemed to be equipped with a notebook and pencil except me.

"Where's your notebook?" George asked in a critical tone.

"I didn't know I was supposed to bring one," I admitted.

"Well, you were!" he whispered heatedly.

To pacify George, I borrowed a stub of a pencil from someone, and thought I'd jot down a few notes on my shirt cuff, just to look as if I wasn't taking this thing lightly.

I thought I'd take a few notes, but before the evening was over the notes extended all the way up my sleeve and down the front of my shirt as well. Lefty was pretty thorough. He covered everything from the Hit and Run to how to decode the opposition's signals.

"Little kids are apt to be plate shy," said Lefty, still going strong exactly three hours and twenty-seven minutes later. "This is on account of kid pitchers don't have much control, and the batter's got a good chance of getting beaned if he isn't careful. But make 'em stand right in there anyway, no matter how frightened they are, on account of they can't get hurt too badly if they're wearing that headgear they make 'em wear these days."

It was obvious that Lefty knew a lot about children, and loved them all.

"One last point," said Lefty, as we breathed sighs of relief. "It's better to let your base runners come sliding in with their spikes flying than to get tagged out because they're afraid of roughing up the baseman. They can't do much harm to a baseman, anyway, with those official little-league rubber spikes," he added, a bit regretfully, I thought.

It was the kind of a lecture that a group of rookies reporting for spring training at St. Petersburg might have a little difficulty absorbing in one sitting. Not that it was giving me any trouble (except when I had to draw a diagram of the Williams Shift on my shirtail). I merely felt that the whole lecture was slightly super-fluous in view of what Roy Harris had told us about *de*-emphasizing winning.

The remaining three weeks preceding the season's opening game were busy ones for George and me.

First of all, there was the uniform situation to get straightened out. George was also sponsoring our team, so he wanted the writing on the shirts to read BROWN'S SANTA MONICA GLASSWORKS & MIRROR COMPANY STARS—OPEN 24 HOURS. I felt that this was too much to make a small boy carry around on his shirt, and I tactfully mentioned it to George.

"Listen," he said, "I'm the one who's investing seventy-five bucks in those uniforms. The least I can do is get the full benefit of the advertising."

George was pretty stubborn about it, but after I argued with him for an hour, he finally agreed to abbreviate the word "Company."

Then there was the job of assigning the players their positions. We called a special tryout session one afternoon after school. It was an alive-looking group of boys who appeared at the Sloping Ravine ball field, carrying sundry baseball equipment and snapping their bubble gum like old pros. There were fifteen of them in all. Most of them, like Steve and Eddie, were nine-year-olds who had never played on an organized team before. But there were a couple of older boys who were veterans of little-league play: Bobby Cordoza, who had pitched a no-hitter for Santa Monica the year previously, and John Ruppert, a catcher.

"I think I'll build the team around them," George confided in me as we watched Cordoza whip a fast ball over the corner of the plate that Ruppert pocketed in his mitt with ease. "Now all we have to do is set the rest of the positions."

It wasn't easy finding the positions for which the other boys were best suited, for most of them weren't suited for anything except chewing bubble gum. Then, too, they all had their own preconceived notions about what positions they wanted to play, and they were reluctant to compromise. However, it wasn't very practical to let them decide, since nine of them wanted to play first base.

Not counting Cordoza and Ruppert we had thirteen boys and only seven positions left to fill. I thought this would present a bit of a problem, but as it turned out, Roy Harris had arranged it this way purposely.

"There'll always be a few who won't show up," he said, "and you won't be able to field a complete team unless you have replacements."

"Supposing they do all show up?" I asked. "Then some won't get to play."

"Not in this league," said Harris firmly. "According to our rules, managers are required to rotate their players so that every kid can participate. But they won't all show. Don't worry."

Because none of the rookies were what you'd call standouts, George decided that the fairest thing to do would be to let all the boys but Ruppert and Cordoza pull their positions out of a hat. This wasn't the way Casey Stengel would have handled it, but at least it was a start.

"We can switch them around until we find the right spots for them," said George.

Steve, to his amazement, got the position he wanted. He drew "alternate pitcher," along with his pal Eddie Brown. We had to have alternate pitchers because Bobby Cordoza, according to little-league rules, could only pitch every other game.

"Whoopee," exclaimed Steve when we arrived home from the field that evening just as Irene was putting the dinner on the table. "I'm going to be pitcher." He took a windup and threw an imaginary fast ball that went right over the plate of lamb stew Irene was serving.

"I'm glad you volunteered to help with the team," said Irene when we were alone. "Steve's getting such a big kick out of it, and it's good for you to get out in the fresh air, too."

It might have been good for me, but I found I had even less time for my own work now than I ever had. During the two weeks that followed, I batted fungoes nearly every afternoon and taught the boys how to field and throw. In the evenings I studied my notes—until Irene accidentally put my shirt with the notes on it in the laundry. I also had to provide free bus service to the field for the boys who couldn't get there on their own. This became necessary when a few of the mothers proved something less than co-operative when it came to seeing that the boys showed up for practice on time, or even at all. They claimed it was interfering with homework and music lessons, orthodontist appointments and even dinner hours. In order to get John Ruppert out, for instance, I had to pick him up at his piano teacher's house, which was ten miles away through dense traffic. I also had to listen to him play, on the days I misjudged the traffic and got there early.

The day of our opening game of the season, against the Los Angeles Graphic Copy & Engraving Co. Angels, dawned bright and clear. I know, because at five o'clock that morning Steve was walking around our bedroom, in full uniform, including spiked shoes, asking when we were leaving for the ball field.

When we did arrive at the field—five hours later—there were some unforeseen complications: all our players showed up. This put George in quite a quandary. Everyone was clamoring in unison, "Let me go in first, Mr. Brown."

George finally decided on a lineup, but it didn't include Steve.

"Cordoza's pitching today," explained George.

"Well, how about letting him play one of the other positions?" I said. "He'd like to get in the game, too."

"He's a pitcher. He'll have to stay in the bull pen in case we need him."

"Eddie's a pitcher, too," I said. "But you've got him on third, I notice."

"I want to see how he does there," said George. "We're a little weak in that position."

We were even weaker in that position after Eddie let four easy grounders get through his legs and roll into the outfield. On his fifth chance, he managed to stop the ball, but he threw it ten feet over the first baseman's head and into the bushes. The game was held up for fifteen minutes while we searched for the ball.

Not that the other players exactly distinguished themselves that day. Maybaum, our centerfielder, after making a fairly good recovery of a line drive, held on to the ball a mite too long, enabling the runner on second to come home. Ruppert, our catcher, threw the ball with all his might at Eddie on third, trying to pick off another runner. But Ruppert overshot Eddie, and the ball sailed out to left field. When another run scored, Ruppert sat down on home plate and started to cry, and nothing George or I could say to him would stop the tears. Fortunately, one of the fathers in the audience happened to be a psychiatrist. He came down out of the bleachers and got Ruppert back on the beam again, so the game could continue (and he only charged us for an office visit).

It was a tribute to Bobby Cordoza's mound wizardry that we were finally able to salvage the game, 19 to 18.

"Well, did you get a home run today?" Irene asked Steve when we walked in the door with Andy, who'd been a spectator at the game.

"He didn't even play," said Andy cheerfully.

"How come?" asked Irene. "I thought they had to use everyone."

"Because pitchers don't get to play in every game," explained Steve, but he was obviously disappointed.

"He'll pitch next game," I assured Irene.

But George had different ideas. "I think I'll start Eddie," he told me before Thursday's game.

"What about Steve?" I asked.

"Oh, I'll use him, too. Maybe I'll rotate them. Let Eddie pitch one inning, and Steve the next, and so on. It'll give them a rest."

Steve had quite a rest that first inning. Eddie walked the first eighteen batters, and beaned three spectators who were sitting with the proud mothers and fathers on benches along the third-base line.

"Don't you think you ought to take him out and put Steve in?" I asked George. Up until then, George had been reluctant to change pitchers, for fear it would be psychologically harmful to

Eddie, but now he was ready to listen to reason. "Okay, Steve, you go in."

"Gee, thanks, Mr. Brown," said Steve, grabbing his glove and racing out to the mound.

He took a very professional looking windup, rearing back just the way I had taught him, and sent a fast ball right over the plate. The batter took a healthy cut at it, and sent a slow dribbler out toward third, where Eddie Brown was playing again. However, it wasn't slow enough, because the ball went through Eddie's legs and out into left field, allowing three more runs to score.

"That's fine pitching," said George, glaring at me.

"He didn't get much help from the third baseman," I reminded him.

"Aw, Eddie never had a chance to get that ball. It took a bad hop."

Steve struck out the next man, but walked the following two. George decided to take him out and try Billy Ziering, the second baseman, on the mound.

I was sorry to see Steve take the long walk to the bench, since it wasn't really his fault that the score was 18 to 0. But the situation did seem to call for desperate measures. Not that we could hope to win. It was just a question of getting the game over with before dark.

We'd already been playing for an hour and twenty minutes, and we were still in the top half of the first inning. True, there's an hour-and-a-half time limit on little-league games, but the ruling can't be invoked until both sides have had their ups.

After Billy Ziering walked the next five batters, George let Maybaum, the centerfielder, take over on the mound. In fact, before the side was finally retired, everyone on the whole squad had pitched, except George and myself.

Finally, Ricky Collins, the shortstop, stepped to the mound and put out the fire. But it was too late. We lost 33 to 0. (Our team's hitting wasn't very sharp that day, either.)

"We're a little weak in the pitching department," said George after the game. George was pretty astute about those things.

"Yes, we are," I said.

"We'll have to improve," muttered George grimly.

"What's the difference?" I said. "The kids are having fun."

"How do you expect to win the championship with that attitude?" exclaimed George. "You ought to be ashamed of yourself."

To get back on his good side, I volunteered to help him work out with Ricky Collins, our new alternate pitcher, every afternoon after school that we didn't have a league game.

While Ricky tried to throw fast balls and curves, floaters and sinkers, I batted, and George read aloud to us from Shorty O'Doul's *Inside Baseball*, Chapter 5, "Pitching."

It was an exhausting ordeal, but it paid off. By mid-season we had pulled all the way up from fourth to third place. We'd actually won two games without Cordoza on the mound.

But though the team was improving slightly, Steve's prospects of getting in the games more often were not. Steve had played a total of four and a half innings so far, and had been up to bat once, which was making him quite bitter about the game of baseball in general, and his manager in particular (and he wasn't too fond of me, either).

Technically, George abided by the rules—in the early part of the season, anyway—and let every boy play at least a half an inning, usually down toward the end of the game, when we either had a safe lead or were hopelessly behind. But as the season progressed, and the games became tight right down to the wire, George, in his anxiety to win, frequently forgot about the boys on the bench entirely. He didn't exactly forget about them, for they were constantly pleading with him to be given a chance, but he'd stall them off until "next inning." And very often, because of the time limit, there'd be no next inning. It was Steve's fate to be a member of the "next-inning" boys on a number of occasions.

However, by a strange coincidence, Eddie Brown was always in the lineup from the beginning, so the time limit couldn't deprive him of his playing privileges.

"Gee whiz, I didn't get to bat again today," Steve complained to me on the way home from one game, in which he'd been allowed to play right field in the last half of the last inning. "Can't *you* do anything about it? I'm as good as Eddie. How come he gets to play so much?"

"Nepotism," I answered.

"What's that mean?"

"It means his father is the manager."

Finally, I had to assert myself with George. "See here," I said to him before the game one day. "How about letting some of the others start for a change?"

"I'd like to," he said, "but they're not dependable."

"But the rules say everyone plays, good or bad."

"Don't bother me with rules," he said. "Can't you see I'm trying to win?"

Steve was in tears when he didn't get into the game at all that day, and he was in hysterics after Andy was quick to point it out to his mother.

"Really, dear, you have to do something," Irene told me in private. "We can't go on this way. Steve is cranky from morning until night. If George is just deliberately ignoring the rules, why can't you tell Roy Harris about it?"

"I don't like to go over people's heads."

"I don't understand such a league," said Irene.

"It's very simple," I explained. "There are just too many players on each team."

"Well, they should have more teams with fewer players on each squad," said Irene. "It was stupid to arrange it this way."

It was a little late to do anything about that, but her suggestion did start me thinking along the right lines.

The idea came to me in a flash when six of the team's mainstays and I were sitting in my car in front of John Ruppert's piano teacher's house on the following Thursday afternoon. Steve wasn't with us, having decided to go straight to the ball field from school, as he was sometimes in the habit of doing, so the idea was immensely practical.

After Ruppert had joined the party, and I had driven up the street, I began having a little engine trouble. The car kept stalling.

After it had happened for the sixth time, I just couldn't seem to get it started again.

"It must be flooded," I told the group. "We'll have to wait a few minutes before I can try it again."

While we were waiting, we dropped into the drug store on the corner, where I treated the boys to Cokes and let them browse through the comic books.

When we finally reached the ball field, the game was three-quarters over. George was a trifle upset over our being delayed, but Steve and some of the other bench warmers, who'd been in the game from the start, were extremely happy.

Of course, I couldn't have engine trouble every time I picked up the group. It might have been suspicious. So before the next game I just happened to detour past the Pacific Palisades 59 Flavors Ice Cream Store.

"Anyone want a little nourishment before the game?" I asked.

"Oh, boy, that would be great," they all screamed in unison.

Was it my fault that they wanted second and third helpings of hot fudge sundaes? After all, they were growing boys.

"Where have you been?" George growled at me when we showed up at the game an hour late.

"We stopped for a little ice cream," I explained. "I guess I forgot to watch the time."

"Well, next time don't stop for ice cream," George shouted at me. "We're in big trouble. Your son just struck out for the third time."

So I couldn't stop for ice cream before the next game. George wouldn't have liked it. But it just so happened I had to stop off at the Pacific Palisades Hobby & Toy Shop, to pick up Steve's electric train engine that was being fixed.

"I have to run in here for a minute," I told the boys. "If you kids want to come along, it's all right with me."

They followed me into the toy store, and before any of us realized it, an hour had passed. It was an expensive hour, too. It cost me thirty dollars. But it was worth it. Ruppert and the other six were extremely pleased with the purchases I had made for them, and they didn't even care much about going into the game when we finally got down to the field.

"Do you mind if I sit this one out, Mr. Brown?" said John Ruppert, winding up the propeller on the rubber-band-powered model airplane I had bought him. "I'd like to try this out before it gets dark."

"Yes, I do mind," said George, glowering at him. "You're first-string catcher. We're not doing a thing with Steve Marx subbing for you."

"He looks like he's doing all right to me," said Ruppert, unconcerned.

"John!" George yelled at him.

"Oh, all right," said Ruppert, reluctantly putting the plane down and starting to strap on his leg protectors.

We won the game, with the six regulars playing the last two innings, but George wasn't at all pleased with my attitude.

"If you ask me," he said, "you're deliberately trying to sabotage the team so I'll have to use Steve. You're not very loyal."

"Well, what of it?" I said. "You've been knowingly breaking the rules by not letting all the boys play in all the games."

"I've been trying to win the championship," said George. "I don't let any personal relationship stand in the way of my having a good team."

"What about Eddie playing every game? He's no better than Steve."

"I use him for a reason. He's shorter than the other players. It's harder for the pitchers to find his strike zone."

"You're playing favorites, and you know it."

"If you don't like the way I'm running things, why don't you go into business for yourself?"

"I think I will. Get yourself a new coach. Steve and I have had enough."

"Good riddance" were Eddie Brown's parting words to Steve.

"Likewise, you little shrimp," Steve yelled to him as we walked off the field.

It was a fitting climax to a game that was allegedly promoting neighborhood friendship and good sportsmanship.

"Well, did you get a home run today?" Irene asked Steve when we walked in the door.

"No, but I did," I said. "I finally told George off, and Steve and I both quit. George'll probably never speak to any of us again."

"I couldn't be happier," said Irene.

I felt that way, too, until the next day when all of Southern California started sweltering under a record heat wave. The temperature rose to 104.

"Can we go swimming at the Browns' today?" asked Steve.

"Of course not. You know I had a fight with Eddie's father."

"Can't you call him up and apologize?"

"Over my dead body," said Irene.

"And mine," I added.

"And mine," said Andy.

"Oh, guy!" said Steve. "I'm hot. I want to go swimming at the Browns', like we used to do."

"Well, you'll just have to suffer with the rest of us," said Irene.

After the heat spell had gone on for another three days, with no letup in sight, Irene said, with an unhappy sigh, "I guess it was a pretty inopportune time to pick a fight with the Browns."

"How'd I know we were going to have a heat wave?"

"Well, you didn't have to pick such a big fight with him, did you?"

"I couldn't help it. It just got out of hand."

"Baseball!" exclaimed Irene. "No wonder the game's in trouble. It's run by a bunch of men."

Even Andy was beginning to rue the day I had taken up baseball.

"You're mean," he told me. "You won't let us go swimming."

I was beginning to doubt that there was anything I could do to save the situation (short of putting in our own pool) when the phone rang on Saturday night, and I answered it.

"This is George," said a desperate-sounding voice. "You've got to come back. The team needs you."

"For what?" I said. "To stand on the sidelines and watch *your* kid play baseball?"

"Forget all that," said George. "Steve can play all he wants. Just come back before it's too late. The team's falling apart without you. We even lost today *with* Cordoza pitching."

"He's entitled to an off day once in a while," I said.

"He wasn't having an off day. He wasn't trying, and neither were the rest of them. They were sulking because I fired you. Before the game they were yelling, 'We want Mr. Marx, or we won't play!'"

"That's very flattering."

"Flattering, hell! It was damn embarrassing having those punks pull a sit-down strike in front of all those people in the stands. And pretty lousy publicity, too, for Brown's Santa Monica Glassworks & Mirror Company."

"Open 24 hours," I said. "Don't forget that."

"Cut it out, will you?" said George. "I finally persuaded them to play today, but Ruppert and a few of the other ringleaders flatly refuse to come back for the next game unless *you* pick them up in *your* car, and take them for an outing before the game."

"You do it. I'm busy."

"They don't want me to do it. They said I'm no fun. Now, come on. We only have six more games left. I'll even let you manage the team, and I'll be the coach."

"I don't know if I shoul—"

"Look," said George, "come over to the pool tomorrow and we'll talk it over. Bring Irene and the kids, and we'll have a barbecue. I'm sure we can work something out."

I was sure we could, too. And we did.

Under my managership, Steve and the rest of the erstwhile bench warmers played as many innings as their more experienced teammates during the remainder of the season.

And if I do say so myself, Steve played brilliantly. He only struck out nine times, he got one hit, a couple of bases on balls, and once he made a beautiful unassisted play in the outfield off a very hard-hit line drive. He didn't catch it, but after the ball disappeared in the bushes, he found it without any assistance from the others.

We didn't win the championship, however. We were squeezed out on the last day in a very hard-fought pitcher's battle, 22 to 21.

But as everybody knows, winning isn't important. What is important is that the children enjoy themselves and have a nice place to swim during the dog days of summer. We were fortunate in having carte-blanche use of the Browns' pool from that time on. The rest of the boys on Browns' Santa Monica Glassworks & Mirror Co. Stars also got the use of the pool for the remainder of the summer. That was part of the deal I made with George.

12

How I Spent a Weekend in Las Vegas

for Hardly Anything (Except Money)

They say that either you're born with the soul of a gambler or else you are not.

Until I spent a weekend in Las Vagas, Nevada, I'd always been firmly convinced that I belonged in the latter category. At least I never had any particular desire to squander the family fortune at the races, and the only passes I knew anything about were the kind you make at girls.

That's why I thought it was foolish of Irene even to suggest Las Vegas when we first started discussing resorts where we could spend a nice, restful, inexpensive weekend.

"We're not gamblers," I protested. "What would we do in a place like Las Vegas?"

"Where have you been hiding?" said Irene exuberantly. "You don't have to gamble to enjoy Las Vegas. Why, fabulous Las Vegas is now considered America's playground!"

She sounded like a travel folder. As a matter of fact, she was reading aloud from one—a brochure sent to us through the mail by the "fabulous Royal Pelican Hotel in *fabulous* Las Vegas."

" 'Besides gambling,' " said Irene, continuing to read aloud from the brochure, " 'the fabulous Royal Pelican offers the discriminating guest swimming, horseback riding, golfing, tennis, walking, dancing or just plain loafing in the desert sun.' "

"What about sunstroke?" I asked. "Does the folder say anything about that?"

"Don't be a comedian," said Irene. "Every place in Vegas is completely air-conditioned. And I understand that the entertainment is out of this world. All the big night-club entertainers go up there and play the hotels. It says here you can see a different show every night, featuring such outstanding talent as Danny Thomas, Joe Lewis, Liberace—"

"I've seen Joe Lewis and Danny Thomas."

". . . and Lili St. Cyr," said Irene, still reading from the folder.

"Well," I said, running and getting my suitcase from the closet, "I suppose I could use some of that invigorating desert air."

"And listen to this," added Irene, turning the brochure over. " 'For the fishing enthusiast, it's only a short drive to Boulder Dam and Lake Mead.' "

"Fishing!" exclaimed Steve. "Oh, boy. I want to go, too. Daddy said he was going to take me fishing again this year. Didn't you, Daddy?"

"No children on this trip," I insisted. "Daddy's been working awfully hard, and he's going away for a rest."

"I need a rest, too," said Andy, throwing himself on the floor and crying hysterically. "I want to go fishing. You never took me."

"I suppose we could take the children," said Irene. "They can go on the plane for half fare."

"Plane?" I exclaimed. "I thought we were going to save money on this trip, and drive someplace."

"Driving through the desert this time of the year is much too hot for the children," pointed out Irene. "I won't hear of it."

"Lili St. Cyr is much too hot for the children, too," I retorted. "What are we going to do with them at night?"

"I don't mind seeing Lili St. Cyr," said Steve.

"Mother will be glad to sit with the children at night," said Irene.

"Mother? ? ? ? !" I yelled.

"Of course, Mother. It'll be a lot cheaper to have her along than to pay out good money for baby sitters."

"But originally we were going to leave them home with *her*, I thought."

"Mother has never seen Las Vegas," said Irene.

"But the expense for five people—plane fare, rooms, food, drinks, magazines, tips! Good God, I'm not made of money."

"Dear, we don't have to pay Mother's way," said Irene with forced patience. "But even if we did it wouldn't be very expensive. Haven't you heard? Las Vegas is the cheapest resort in the world to go to. The people who run the hotels make so much money from the gambling that they can afford to give the rooms and food away for practically nothing, just to get you up there. So all we have to do is stay away from the gambling rooms, and the trip will be such a bargain that we can't afford *not* to go."

So we went.

On Friday afternoon a DC-6 bearing four Marxes and one mother-in-law swooped down out of the clouds over Las Vegas' sun-baked airport. The five of us trooped out of the airplane and waited in front of the terminal for our bags.

"Taxi, mister?" shouted a cab driver, while we stood there, breathing in the healthful desert air, which felt something like the blast from a furnace, only not as cool.

I explained to him that it would probably take a few minutes for our baggage to be unloaded from the plane, and that I didn't want to tie him up that long.

"Oh, that's all right," he said politely. "I'll wait."

He hopped out of his cab and quickly relieved me of the many objects I had been juggling in my arms since we had alighted from the plane: Irene's overcoat and cosmetic kit, Grace's crossword-puzzle book, Steve's fishing pole, a small but heavy tractor made of solid lead belonging to Andy, and a complete Davy Crockett outfit, including powder horn and musket, that Steve had insisted I buy him on our way through the terminal.

As I watched the cab driver deposit our paraphernalia in the back seat of his taxi, and settle down behind the steering wheel to wait for our bags (which took almost as long as the plane ride itself), I was impressed, I must admit, with how friendly and eager to be helpful the man was.

I realized why, when the bags finally arrived and we were piling into the back seat of the taxi. Our cab hadn't moved yet, but the meter already read $2.38.

"What's the idea?" I said. "You're not supposed to start the meter until we're ready to go. This is an outrage."

"What's the difference?" said the driver, with a shrug. "You might as well spend the money on me as throw it away in those casinos. At least I'm giving you a ride for your money."

It wasn't much of a ride. The Royal Pelican Hotel, where Irene had made reservations, was only a mile from the airport. By the time we reached there, the meter read four dollars, and the driver added an extra fifty cents for two of us, claiming that his legal load was only three people.

However, I didn't argue with him. I figured I could afford to let him gyp me. After all, the hotel accommodations were going to cost us practically nothing, and we weren't going to do any gambling. Oh, we might put a few nickels into a slot machine, provided we had a few minutes to kill, but no gambling to speak of.

I flashed a twenty-dollar bill in front of the cab driver. "Got change?" I asked.

"Have I got change!" he said.

He dropped fifteen silver dollars into my palm.

"I can't put all these cartwheels into my wallet," I said. "Don't you have any paper money?"

"In this town?" He doubled up with laughter. "You must be kidding!" he said, and he got back into his cab and drove away.

Staggering under the weight of so much silver, I followed my entourage into the lobby of the Royal Pelican.

My eyes found it a little difficult to make the adjustment as I went from the blinding desert sunlight into the murky, smoke-filled atmosphere of the Royal Pelican. But after I blinked a dozen or so times, and wiped the nicotine out of my eyes with a handkerchief, I managed to overcome my temporary blindness, and I strode up to the room clerk.

"My name's Arthur Marx," I announced. "I have a reservation here for five people for the weekend."

"Ten'll get you twenty you don't," he muttered, casually shuffling a deck of cards.

"Isn't this the fabulous Royal Pelican?" I asked.

"Yeah, but this is the blackjack table," he said, "and I'm a dealer. I ain't no crummy room clerk. The desk is over there."

He pointed to the other side of the lobby.

Apologizing profusely, I proceeded to thread my way across the lobby through a maze of slot machines, roulette wheels and crap tables, all of which were doing a land-office business, even though it was only four in the afternoon.

As I stopped in front of the room clerk's counter, Irene and the children and Grace suddenly appeared at my elbow.

"Oh, there you are," said Irene. "I've been looking all over for you. Where have you been?"

"Daddy?" asked Steve. "Can I have a nickel for a slot machine?"

"I want a slot machine, too!" cried Andy.

"I was paying the taxi driver," I explained to Irene.

"Well, I hope you don't mind. I went ahead and registered."

"I don't mind," I said, as the bellhop led us to our suite of three connecting rooms on the second floor.

I didn't mind, that is, until, when I was unpacking, I discovered a card, tacked to the inside of our closet door, giving the room rates.

"Twenty bucks a day!" I exclaimed. "There must be some mistake."

"Well, they had some rooms for only sixteen a day," replied Irene, "but the clerk said we wouldn't like those. They're right over the kitchen, and you can hear the help rattling dishes and pots and pans early in the morning."

I decided not to argue about it. It would be worth four dollars a day extra to be able to sleep late in the mornings. Besides, the room had a nice view of the swimming pool, and it was luxuriously appointed.

In fact the ultra-modern furnishings looked so comfortable that I decided to stretch out on the bed and take a short nap.

"Let's all take a short nap," said Irene, "and then we'll go for a swim."

As I sat down on the bed to take my shoes off, I felt an icy draft on the back of my neck. The blast seemed to be coming from a vent in the wall.

"It's awfully cold in here," I said.

"It's the air conditioning," said Irene, rubbing her hands together briskly to keep her blood circulating. "Maybe you ought to turn it down a little."

Unfortunately, there didn't seem to be any way of adjusting the air conditioning, short of turning it off entirely. And when I tried that, the heat turned on automatically and the five of us almost suffocated to death, because the windows were sealed closed to keep the air from the air conditioner from escaping.

Even the bellboy whom the room clerk sent up to adjust our air conditioner was powerless to do anything. "Look, mister," he explained, "your air conditioner is either on or off. When it's on, it's cold in here, and when it's off, it's hot. It's as simple as that. Understand?"

In exchange for that pearl of wisdom I tipped him a silver dollar, having no United States currency left on me, and went back to trying to figure out the air-conditioning system myself.

"I think I'll go play some Bingo," announced Grace, emerging from her room in a sunsuit. "I understand there's a place in town offering two five-hundred-dollar pots."

"While you're working on the air conditioner," said Irene, "I think I'll take the children for a dip in the pool. They're getting restless."

I was getting restless, too, but of course, somebody had to do the dirty work.

It took me the remainder of the afternoon to discover that the bellboy was right—there was no happy medium. It was either shiver or suffocate.

I chose the former, as the best of two horrible alternatives, and turned my thoughts to what we would do about dinner, since it was six o'clock by then and Irene and the children were back, all claiming to be famished from their invigorating workout in the pool.

"I suggest that your mother and the children eat up here in the room," I told Irene, "while you and I sneak over to the Sahara where Lili St. Cyr is playing, and dine in style."

It was an excellent plan, except for two things: (1) Lili St. Cyr was no longer at the Sahara, or anywhere else in town, for that matter. And (2) no one knew what had become of Irene's mother.

She was last seen heading for the Showboat Bingo Parlor, about seven miles away, but when I went there in a taxi searching for her, at a quarter after seven, she had gone on to another Bingo parlor, but nobody seemed to know which one.

"A fine thing," I complained to Irene when I returned to our room, where Steve and Andy were just finishing a well-balanced supper of hot dogs, French-fried potatoes and Cokes. "We let your mother come along so she can baby-sit for us. And what happens? She disappears when we need her the most."

"Well, she didn't promise to baby-sit *all* the time," Irene now revealed. "Let her have her fun. Maybe the bell captain can get us a regular baby sitter."

In the lobby, I found the head bell captain, who looked like a cross between Nick the Greek and Gaylord Ravenal.

"My wife and I would like a baby sitter for tonight," I said, slipping a silver dollar into his palm the way I'd seen other big operators handle similar situations in the movies.

"You and seven hundred other people," said the bell captain scornfully. "Haven't you heard? This is Friday night, and you're in Las Vegas."

Before pocketing my silver dollar, he looked at it rather disdainfully, and then started to walk away. I got the hint and crossed his palm with another piece of silver.

"Well, now," he said, jingling a whole pocketful of silver, "maybe I can think of someone to sit with your kids, if you'll just give me some time to think. My memory's a little fuzzy right at the moment."

By the time I had unburdened myself of five more silver dollars, the bell captain's thinking powers had made a remarkable recovery. He picked up a phone, and, within a matter of seconds, was able to get hold of one of the hotel's chambermaids, who doubled in baby sitting.

The baby sitter, whose name was Nellie Butterworth, wasn't much to look at, but she seemed like a pleasant old lady, and, what was more important, her rates were low. She only charged fifty cents an hour, which was lower than the baby-sitting rates in Los Angeles. However, she hastily explained, she had a ten-hour minimum charge. But we were too hungry to quibble about a thing like that.

Congratulating ourselves on having secured a baby sitter at all, Irene and I headed for the main dining room. What if we weren't going to see Lili St. Cyr? At least we'd get a drink and a good steak dinner, and we'd see some kind of a floor show, according to the poster in the lobby, which advertised a line-up of beautiful Copa girls and a singing group called the Four Sons of the Sahara.

"Do you have a reservation?" asked the maître de.

"No. But we're guests of the hotel," I said.

"Sorry," he said. "All filled up for tonight."

"I don't want to see the Four Sons of the Sahara, anyway," said Irene. "Let's go someplace else."

We found a cab, and made the rounds of all the hotels and first-class eating spots in town. But it was the same story everywhere. You couldn't get in without a reservation, or pull, and we didn't have either.

At nine-thirty, hungry, weary and ten dollars poorer because of the cab fare, we wound up back at the "fabulous" Royal Pelican, discussing our problem with the always helpful head bell captain.

"Why don't you grab a sandwich in the coffee shop?" he suggested. "I think you can get a table in there. If not, there's always room at the counter."

"We didn't come all the way to Las Vegas to eat at a counter," said Irene.

The bell captain shrugged. "Friday night, you know. It's pretty difficult. But why don't you be smart and let me get you a reservation someplace for tomorrow night?" he said, holding out his hand.

"Okay. We'll be smart," I said, dropping a dollar into the hand.

"How about Rosemary Clooney?" he said. "Would you like to go and see her tomorrow night? She's at the Sands."

"That would be fine," said Irene. "She's my favorite singer."

"I'll have to put you on my waiting list, though—she's awfully popular," said the captain, jingling the change in his pockets.

I handed him three more silver dollars. "Now how popular is Rosemary Clooney?"

"I just got a hot flash," he said, pocketing the money. "A couple from Grand Rapids who were going to see Rosemary Clooney tomorrow night just called up and cancelled, and I can take you off the waiting list."

Irene and I were in a reckless mood by the time we finished dinner in the coffee shop and were walking back through the casino.

"As long as we can't get into a show tonight," said Irene, stopping in front of a nickel slot machine and opening her purse, "why don't we play the slot machines for a while?"

"I don't know if that's a good idea," I said. "I've heard that once you start on those things, you never stop until you're broke."

"Don't be a square," said Irene. "There's no reason why a person can't gamble sensibly. We'll put a limit on how much we'll lose—like a dollar each—and when that's gone, we'll go to bed." She dropped a nickel into the slot and yanked hard on the arm. "Besides, I feel lucky tonight."

Her hunch proved correct. The slot machine stopped on two cherries and a bust of John Dillinger. Five nickels came sliding out the bottom.

"See, what did I tell you?" exclaimed Irene jubilantly. "There's nothing to it."

It did look like a ridiculously simple way to make money, even I had to admit. And it certainly had it all over writing. Anyway, you couldn't really lose much just putting nickels into a machine, and there was always a chance that you'd win a jackpot.

I felt around in my pockets for some loose nickels, and when I couldn't find any, I stepped fearlessly to the cashier's cage.

"Give me a dollar's worth of nickels," I said as matter-of-factly as if I had been buying a package of gum.

Armed with my gambling limit for the evening, I stopped at the machine next to the one Irene was playing, put a nickel into the slot and pulled the lever.

Wouldn't it be amusing, I thought as I watched the wheels go round, if I won the jackpot on my very first try? And wouldn't Irene, with the lousy five nickels she had just won, be terribly envious of my knack for gambling?

Both of these questions turned out to be purely academic, because all that turned up on my machine were three lemons.

I knew, of course, that I was being a Walter Mitty to dream that I would win the jackpot on my first attempt, or even on my second or third attempts. But after I had made twenty straight attempts, and the machine hadn't coughed up a single nickel, I didn't know what I was being. I suspected that I was being a sucker, and that I ought to quit, because no one could beat the slot machines. After all, they weren't called "one-armed bandits" for nothing.

However, I was out too much money already to quit now. I'd first have to recoup my losses, which would be just a matter of time. As I explained to Irene, I had a feeling that the machine was due to pay off—and big—any minute now. And it would be shortsighted of me to leave all that money there, just waiting for someone else to come along and win it on the first try.

"While you're at it, get me some nickels too," said Irene, as I departed for the cashier's cage to get more change. "I don't want to be shortsighted, either."

By not being shortsighted, the two of us managed to drop another ten dollars in the slot machines by the time we departed for our room at one A.M. Of course, we had done just what we had said we wouldn't do—we hadn't stopped when we had exceeded our limit—but it would hardly have paid us to return to our room earlier, in view of Nellie Butterworth's ten-hour minimum charge.

We tiptoed through our room on our way to the children's room, so we wouldn't wake them up. But it turned out that they weren't even in bed.

Steve and Andy were seated on the floor, listening avidly to Nellie Butterworth, who was down on her hands and knees, teaching them the rudiments of the game of craps with a pair of dice she had brought along to keep her young charges amused.

However, she must not have done a very good job of teaching them, because in addition to her baby-sitting fees I wound up having to pay her another seven dollars which she claimed Steve had lost by crapping out nine times in a row. (I had a good mind not to pay her this, and I wouldn't have, except I was afraid she might get mad and not come back to work for us the following night. And I had a hunch we were going to need her, because Grace still hadn't returned from the Bingo parlor.)

Irene and I went to bed, having made up our minds that the gambling casino had seen the last of us. We'd learned our lesson; we'd leave the games of chance to the people who didn't know any better. From now on, we'd stick to the more healthful activities that Las Vegas had to offer—swimming and sun bathing, for instance.

There was only one trouble with that plan. When we awoke in the morning, a small gale was blowing outside our window. And by after lunch, the wind was whipping up such a sandstorm that even a full-blooded Arab wouldn't have dared venture outside the hotel.

"Well, I don't know about you," said Irene, "but I'm not going swimming in this weather."

"Me, neither," I said. "And I don't think the kids should."

"Well, what *are* we going to do?" cried Steve, bursting into tears. "You said we could go fishing one day. Why don't we do that?"

"It's too windy for fishing, too," I said. "Maybe your Nanny will read you a story." I looked Grace right in the eye.

"Not now," said Grace, glancing anxiously at her watch. "I've got to get right over to the Showboat. At two o'clock they're going to start the game with the fifty-dollar pot. And after that I have to go over and see Nat King Cole at his hotel. I think I may land him on a new song I've written."

We finally pacified the children by promising to take them downstairs to the casino and let them each put a quarter's worth of nickels into the slot machines. But no sooner had we arrived in the casino and Steve started to reach up and put a nickel in the slot machine than a husky, uniformed guard approached us with an unfriendly glint in his eye.

"Get those kids out of here," he snarled. "Don't you know it's against the law for them even to be in the casino? Do you want us to lose our license?"

For a moment I thought he was going to draw his gun, but he was only resting his hand on the pistol butt.

"Maybe I'll take the children for a ride downtown," said Irene, after the bouncer had escorted us all the way out of the casino and stood there to make sure we didn't try to return. "I understand there are some nice shops on the main street."

The only other alternative was for them to go swimming in the sandstorm, but this didn't get a very friendly response from Irene when I suggested it, so I had to let them go. Besides, it would give me an opportunity to mosey around the casino by myself.

Of course, I had no intention of doing any gambling myself when I stopped at the least crowded of the crap tables to watch a short man in a ten-gallon Stetson throwing the dice. I was merely curious to see how the game was played.

After watching a few minutes, I was surprised that there was so little to the ancient and honorable game of craps. Not only did it appear simple, but judging from what I had seen, the house didn't have much of an advantage over the customers. All you had to do was throw a seven or an eleven on your first throw, and you received twice your money back. And if you were trying for your point, you had as many chances as you wanted to make it—provided you didn't throw a seven first.

It seemed fair enough. And certainly the odds weren't thirty-seven to one against you, as they were in roulette.

Or if you really wanted to be safe, you could play along with the house while the other fellow was shooting, and put your money on the "no-pass" line.

Just to test my theory—purely for scientific purposes—I put one silver dollar on the no-pass line when it was the next shooter's roll, and, sure enough, he failed to make his point and I received two dollars for my one.

As I suspected, this game was a cinch—if you knew how to play it. And I knew how to play it.

I pocketed one of the dollars, and left the other on the no-pass line. None of that doubling up for me. From now on, I'd be playing with the house's money. How could I lose?

Another shooter failed to make his point, and I was another dollar to the good. I had won twice in a row!

I could hardly believe my good fortune. I was a success. Others might have failed, but I had somehow figured out a system for breaking the bank. This was a lot quicker way of making money than by playing those crooked slot machines. Slot machines were for women. Craps was a man's game.

I spent the rest of the afternoon playing the no-pass line, and wisely declining to roll the dice myself. At five-thirty, when I quit and went up to our room, I was twenty-seven dollars ahead of the game—almost enough to pay for the dress Irene had bought that afternoon.

But what did I care that she had squandered away my hard-earned winnings in a dress shop in downtown Las Vegas? I could afford to be generous, because I had stumbled upon a foolproof system for beating the crap table—a system that I would put to a more serious test later in the evening, after we had eaten and drunk our fill at the Sands Hotel, and been royally entertained by Rosemary Clooney and thirty-seven beautiful Copa girls.

The maître de at the Sands Hotel seemed slightly mystified when Irene and I showed up at the entrance of the Desert Paradise Room at seven-forty-five to claim our reservation that the bell captain at the Royal Pelican had supposedly made for us the previous evening, and for which I had tipped him so generously.

"Marx?" he said, looking down his list. "I don't have any reservations under the name Marx. Are you sure?"

"Of course I'm sure—my name's always been Marx," I said. "And I know I have a reservation because I was standing right beside the head bell captain at the Royal Pelican last night when he phoned you and made it."

"Oh, so you're the party," said the maître de, with an enlightened look. "Well, no wonder. I thought he meant the reservation was for last night. Sorry, sir, but we're all booked up for tonight. But perhaps I could squeeze you in somewhere if—"

He knew what he was talking about when he used the word "squeeze."

First he squeezed a rather large tip out of me, and then he seated us at a table for one that was squeezed in between two tables for twelve, which in turn were squeezed in between a row of phony palm trees and the wall that was farthest away from the stage.

We never did find out what Rosemary Clooney or the thirty-seven beautiful Copa girls looked like, because we couldn't see them through the palm trees. Occasionally I got a glimpse of the left arm and left leg of one Copa girl—the one who was on the extreme end of the line—but it was hardly worth the expense I'd gone to just to get a table.

As a matter of fact, we couldn't even see what our steaks looked like, because they weren't served to us until after the floor show began and the lights were turned off. In the darkness, a bus boy, who apparently had us confused with another party who were just finishing, cleared away our dinner dishes before we had taken more than a couple of bites.

The lights were turned on again just in time for us to see the check which the waitress brought us the moment Rosemary Clooney closed her lips on the last note of her last encore.

"We haven't finished our coffee," I objected.

"Sorry, sir," exclaimed the waitress, "but we have to start cleaning up so we can start seating people for the second show."

I was pleased about one thing, anyway. As I had heard, it was really true that none of the night spots in Las Vegas had a cover charge. Because of the gambling they could give you all that entertainment for nothing.

Of course, the cheapest item on the menu was six and a half dollars—shrimp cocktail seventy-five cents extra—and two people would be doing extremely well to get away for less than twenty dollars. But there was *no* cover charge.

Actually, I didn't care that they had hustled us out of the dining room so fast, because what I wanted to do the most was to get back to the Royal Pelican and try out my system again at the dice table.

"Just wait until you see me in action," I told Irene, as I stepped up to the same table where I had been so lucky that afternoon, and bought twenty silver dollars. "I'm going to win enough right now to pay for the whole trip."

"Are you crazy?" said Irene. "I thought nickel slot machines were our speed."

"Slot machines are for women and suckers," I explained. "This is the game to play if you want to make real money fast. Just watch me. I've got a system."

I put a dollar on the no-pass line, and again my strategy paid off. In fact, it paid off five times in a row. By then Irene was beginning to have some respect for my prowess as a gambler.

"Gee, this is wonderful!" she exclaimed, gazing at the stack of silver dollars in front of me. "Give me some of those, dear. I might as well get in on this killing, too."

I gave her half of my loot, and the two of us settled down to the serious business of breaking the bank.

We were doing all right too—or rather, I thought we were doing all right—until I discovered that for every dollar I had put on

151

the no-pass line, Irene had put one on the pass line. Instead of being twenty dollars ahead, we were exactly even.

"You dope," I said. "How can we make any money if you're betting against me?"

"Don't call me a dope," she said. "And I wasn't betting against *you*. I was merely betting that that nice man over there in the plaid sport jacket would make his point."

Time was called while I explained to Irene that betting on someone else was the same as betting against me. "You know," I said, "united we stand, divided we fall. Put your money on the no-pass line like I do."

United we fell, too. With Irene playing the no-pass line along with me, everyone else at the table suddenly got lucky. One fellow threw nine straight passes, which just about cleaned us out of the twenty dollars we had begun with.

"That's what we get for betting *against* everyone else," said Irene remorsefully. "It serves us right. It was against my better instincts in the first place."

It was at this point that Speed Allen, an old-time riverboat gambler I had once met in Hollywood, sidled up to me and said out of the corner of his mouth, "Don't play that table, you schmo. It ain't hot! Find yourself a hot table, or else quit."

"What's a hot table?" I asked.

He looked at me unbelievingly. "You don't know what's a hot table?"

I shook my head guiltily.

"Schmo," said Allen. "A hot table is one where the customers are beating the house. You've got to find one of them and start putting your money on the pass line. You'll clean up."

"How do I recognize a hot table?" I asked.

"Just keeping walking around until you hear a lot of 'Ahs' and 'Ohs' and screams of excitement. That means someone's having a hot run at one of the tables. Find that table and start laying your dough on the line as fast as you can."

He suddenly put a hand to his ear, and listened. "Shhhh, I think I hear a table warming up now," he said.

We listened, and we could hear screams of excitement coming from a table across the room.

"That's our spot," said Allen, starting to pull us toward the hot table. "Let's get over there before it cools off."

There was such a large crowd gathered around the table that it appeared, for an anxious moment, as if there wouldn't be room for the three of us. But luckily, three people suddenly pulled out guns and shot themselves simultaneously, so we were able to squeeze in.

Irene and I each put a dollar on the pass line. Allen scowled at us.

"Are you two mad—betting dollars on a *hot* table?" he said scornfully. "Get yourself some of these"—he held up a handful of five-dollar chips—"and make yourself some real dough while the opportunity is yours."

It sounded like such a sure thing that I didn't hesitate a moment when Allen advised me to buy a hundred dollars' worth of five-dollar chips, and bet the same as he was betting.

I blew myself to a hundred dollars' worth of chips and, following Allen's example, put twenty-five dollars' worth on the pass line.

"Arthur," exclaimed Irene, frightened, "what's got into you—throwing money around like that?"

"I'm not throwing money around," I replied. "Didn't you hear what he said about making money while the opportunity was ours?"

"Come on—hard six!" shouted a cowboy who had a huge stack of ten-dollar chips in front of him, and who was shaking the dice in his hand. "Come on, baby needs a new Cadillac."

He tossed the dice and they galloped across the table.

Seven!

As I went pale and Irene looked angrily at me, the croupier calmly raked in all the chips that were on the pass line.

After that fiasco, I hesitated about putting any more five-dollar chips down, but my friend said, "Don't chicken out on a hot table—just because you were unlucky once. The odds are all with you. Let's double up, and be ahead of the game this time."

He put fifty on the pass line, and, because I couldn't afford not to, I did the same.

This time the shooter led off with boxcars. Again I lost my money.

"I guess this table has cooled off," said Allen, picking up his remaining chips. "Sometimes by the time you get to a table that's hot you're too late. See you later." He disappeared into the bar.

With my remaining twenty-five dollars I decided to go back to my old system of playing the no-pass line. It had worked pretty well that afternoon. Maybe I could recoup some of my losses.

However, the dice must have overheard me telling my plan to Irene, because as soon as I started playing the no-pass line a shooter came along who threw three sevens and two elevens in a row, breaking me.

"How could you do such a thing?" lamented Irene, after we had returned to our room, paid off Nellie Butterworth, and were getting into bed. "Throwing away a hundred dollars on the crap table. Couldn't you have played with single dollars instead of fives? Who do you think you are—Nick the Greek?"

"Let's not fight about it," I said. "It was your idea to come to Vegas. So what if we did lose a couple of hundred dollars? We might have made a fortune."

"Yes, I guess you're right," yawned Irene. "So what's the difference? We didn't come here to make money. We came here for a rest. Tomorrow we'll sleep late, go swimming with the kids and take an afternoon plane home."

It sounded good—especially the part about sleeping late. So we left a note on Grace's bed, telling her to get the children up in the morning (we were hopeful that she'd be back from the Bingo parlor by then), and after that we turned off the lights.

But a party was going on in the room above ours, and the merrymakers didn't quiet down until four o'clock. Between their noises and the insomnia I had from worrying about the money I had spent on this one weekend, I didn't drop off to sleep until five A.M.

At five-fifteen a thunderous explosion shook the whole hotel—

my bed in particular—and shattered a few windows.

"What's that?" said Irene, sitting up in bed.

"I don't know," I said. "Maybe the guest next door shot himself."

I picked up the phone and reported the disturbance to the room clerk.

"Noise?" he said. "Oh, that!" He chuckled heartily. "Oh, that was just another A-bomb going off. They're having big doings again over at Yucca Flats this morning. Government's blowing up a whole town."

So if you want a nice, restful, inexpensive weekend, do as it tells you to do in the brochure from the fabulous Royal Pelican Hotel —go to fabulous Las Vegas.

13

Jack of All Instruments

One of the problems of child raising which is not included in books on the subject is Musicianship, or How to Get Your Little Would-Be Heifetzes and Rubinsteins to Practice. It's not included for a very obvious reason: no adult has yet found a way to cope with this touchy problem.

Just how ill-equipped the average parent is to handle this stickler is evidenced by the great number of your own generation you meet in living rooms who say boastfully, "I took piano lessons when I was a kid, and I can't play a note today." Actually, they are just being modest. After a couple of martinis, they can usually be coaxed into sitting down at the piano and stumbling through a few measures of one of their old pieces—usually Beethoven's "Minuet in G." When this musical mayhem is over they will then say (if there's anyone left to say it to), "I don't know *why* I didn't keep my music up."

Irene and I (both past masters of the "Minuet in G" ourselves) were determined that Steve wouldn't wind up making a fool of *him*self at parties.

We knew that Steve was gifted musically, because his grandmother, who used to play the piano professionally, told us so. I remember the night we discovered he was a musical genius. Grace had dined with us, and while the three of us were having our coffee, we heard strange sounds emanating from the piano in the living room. It could have been our cat walking up and down the keyboard. But it wasn't—we didn't have a cat.

"It's me, Nanny—I'm playing," Steve called out from the living room. "Aren't I good?"

"That's marvelous!" Grace called back to him. Then to us she added, "You know, he really has a feeling for music—I can tell. I believe he's trying to pick out a song. You *must* give him lessons!"

"I think so, too," said Irene, who's still under her mother's spell at the grand old age of ——.

Irene spent the next week interviewing prospective piano teachers and worrying over which one to take.

Personally, I couldn't see that it made much difference. From what I've been able to observe, most music teachers are strangely similar. They wear large-brimmed hats, and carry lots of gold stars around in their bulging purses. They have a remarkable facility for keeping you completely in the dark about their own playing ability. And they are usually quick to assure you that your child is potentially a combination of Horowitz, Liberace and Oscar Levant.

Irene finally decided on Mrs. McGinley, who bustled into the house one afternoon with a copy of *Teaching Little Fingers to Play* under her arm. "Now, if I don't think your boy has it in him to learn, I'll tell you," she said, while Steve was squirming on the piano bench, eager to get started. "No use wasting your money, or my time."

Irene and I were a little on edge as we waited for Mrs. McGinley to give us her honest opinion. But we needn't have worried. I could tell Steve had made the grade from the smile of pure rapture on Mrs. McGinley's face when the first lesson was finished (and I was taking out my wallet to pay her).

"This young man is loaded with musical talent," she revealed. "And he has perfect hands for the piano, too. Would you like to show Mommy and Daddy what we learned today, Stevey?"

"Sure." Steve placed his right hand on Middle C and rattled off "Up the Hill and Down the Hill" like I've never heard it played before.

"And Steve has promised me he's going to practice every day, so he can get lots of gold stars," said Mrs. McGinley. "Haven't you, Steve?"

"Yes, ma'am. I'll love practicing."

I thought this was just an idle boast, but Steve surprised us. During the next seven days he covered about a hundred miles on his many travels "Up the Hill and Down the Hill."

"He's improving amazingly fast," Mrs. McGinley told us after the second lesson, as she licked a handful of gold stars and plastered them all over the music book and the front of the piano (she was slightly nearsighted). "I'm very proud of this young man. I tell you this in the strictest confidence, but he makes some of my other pupils look sick."

Steve must have felt some remorse about putting her other pupils in a bad light, for he didn't practice quite so hard between the second and third lessons. In fact, several times Irene had to prod him into practicing.

"I only heard you play 'Scaling the Wall' once today," she told him one afternoon. "Didn't Mrs. McGinley say you should play it three times every day?"

"I played it the other two times when you were out to the store."

By the fifth week, Steve was making no attempt to deceive us.

"Did you practice today?" I asked.

"I couldn't. I had a Den Meeting. Guy, I don't have time for *everything*."

"Horowitz found time to practice."

"He doesn't belong to the Cub Scouts—at least he's not in my Den."

Steve didn't abandon his musical career completely. Occasionally he'd sit down at the piano—on his way through the living room—and run through "Up the Hill and Down the Hill," for old times' sake. But his burning enthusiasm for the instrument seemed to have expired.

After several months, Irene decided on a more forceful approach. "Your daddy and I are going to stop the piano lessons if you don't start practicing regularly," she warned Steve. "How would you like that?"

"I'd like it fine," said Steve. (That'll teach you to make threatening remarks to your children.)

"Oh, come on," pleaded Irene. "You don't really want to quit, do you? Don't you want to be able to play an instrument?"

"Yeah, but not the piano—I want to play the violin!" he suddenly blurted out. "Then I can be in the school orchestra. They already have a piano player, but they need violins. And they'll teach me. And I can carry my violin on the school bus, like the other orchestra kids do."

"You won't have any more time to practice the violin than you do the piano," I pointed out.

"Sure, I will, because I *want* to play the violin," he said. "I never did like the piano very much."

Since we didn't feel like investing in a violin until we could be sure he'd stick to it, Irene rented one from the school. It was a pretty tired-looking instrument, but in Steve's eyes it was a Stradivarius. The first night he had it home, he took it to bed with him, case and all.

The next afternoon he came home from school with the announcement that he had made the Canyon School Orchestra. (This will give you an idea of the orchestra.)

"I think I'll get him a violin teacher, so he can learn correctly," Irene said one night. "Steve tells me they don't get much personal instruction in orchestra."

A few days later, a Mrs. Stone came to the house. She was approximately the same woman as Mrs. McGinley, only the brim of her hat was a little floppier, and she carried a violin.

"This young man has splendid hands for the fiddle," she informed us in a high-pitched voice, after listening to Steve saw his way through one of his orchestra pieces. "And he has a good ear, too."

Under Mrs. Stone's tutelage, Steve made rapid strides. Within a week he could tune up by himself. Within a month he could get almost as much resin on his bow as he could on the carpet. And within two months he could hold the fiddle under his chin without using his hands. He could also play one piece—"Dark Eyes"

—well enough to make me believe, if I closed my eyes, that I was in a broken-down gypsy restaurant.

Steve seemed well on his way to becoming a pit musician at the Radio City Music Hall, when a familiar problem started cropping up again. One day I realized I hadn't heard the familiar squeaking and scratching of his violin for a whole week. However, this time Irene and I decided to put the problem squarely up to his teacher, who at least was getting paid to make a musician out of him.

"Yes, I have a splendid system for making boys practice," said Mrs. Stone after the next lesson, which even she admitted had been a fiasco. "For every day that he doesn't practice, deduct a nickel from his allowance."

"He doesn't get that much," I said.

"I have a better idea," said Irene. "We'll give him a nickel for every day that he *does* practice."

"Make it a dime and I'll take it," bargained Steve.

For a dime a session, Steve was confident he could find plenty of time to practice (proof of the power of positive thinking). The time he decided on was early in the morning, before he left for school.

"Oh, no," I protested. "If he's going to get paid for it, he can find time to practice when the rest of us aren't sleeping."

"He won't wake you up," said Irene. "He can take his violin to the other end of the house, so you can't hear him."

It seemed logical, until six o'clock the next morning, when I heard someone playing the piano.

"What's he doing that for?" I yelled, jumping out of bed.

"He's just using the piano to tune up," said Irene. "It won't take long."

He had barely got the violin in tune when it was time to stop practicing and get ready for school. This went on every day for a month. (The violin, I found to my dismay, had to be tuned anew each morning.)

Fortunately, while Steve was tuning up one morning he broke

one of the strings. I had a two-day respite before Irene got around to buying him a new one.

In fact, I had a number of brief respites after that. Something was always happening to the violin. At frequent intervals, Steve snapped each of the strings. Then he broke the bridge. After we replaced the bridge, all the horsehairs on Steve's bow snapped. At first he claimed it had happened while he was playing "The Emperor Waltz." But under interrogation he confessed that he'd been using his bow for a fencing foil in a hand-to-hand encounter with Andy, whose weapon was a toy shovel. The bow snapped while he was trying to parry one of Andy's thrusts. "So it's all Andy's fault," said Steve, logically. "He was playing too rough."

By now I was becoming suspicious of all Steve's "accidents" with his violin. This suspicion was strengthened when I learned that Irene was still paying Steve his dime a day even when his violin was unplayable. She refused to believe that such an ardent music lover would stoop to such chicanery as deliberately putting the violin out of commission (Oedipus Rex raising his ugly head again).

"Mrs. Stone said it's just a very poor-grade violin he's renting," Irene told me. "That's why it keeps breaking. I think we should buy him a decent one. It would give him an incentive."

"I think we shouldn't," I said. "Those things are expensive, and he doesn't seem to be as interested in playing as he used to be."

The subject was dropped—until Christmastime. Then I fell easy prey.

"We don't know what else to get Steve, anyway," said Irene. "And we're getting Andy a bicycle. So let's give Steve a violin. It'll be a nice surprise on Christmas morning."

A couple of days before Christmas Irene brought home a violin, all gift wrapped, and hid it in my closet. It made a very impressive-looking gift, and I was glad we'd bought it for him—until early the next morning, when I heard some very distressing sounds coming from the living room. Steve was playing the piano, and going at it with a vengeance.

"Guess what?" said Steve, at the breakfast table. "I think I like the piano better after all. I'm going back to it."

Irene smiled wanly. "But you're doing so nicely on the violin, dear. Why go back to the piano now?"

"It's more fun!"

"What about the orchestra?" I said. "You can't just walk off and leave them without a first desk man."

"Oh, they have plenty of violinists," Steve assured me.

We couldn't let our investment in the violin go to waste, so we resorted to one final persuasive measure—we revealed what his Christmas present was. Irene even brought it out of the closet to show it to him.

"Oh, boy," said Steve, plucking a string. "This is keen!"

"You don't want to go back to the piano *now*, do you?" said Irene hopefully.

"Well"—Steve thought for a moment, then said, smilingly, "I have a good idea. Why can't I take both?"

"Ridiculous!" I said.

"Why is it ridiculous?" said Irene. "Lots of professional musicians double up. *They* must have taken two kinds of lessons."

"They also found time to practice two instruments," I said.

"I'll practice both," pleaded Steve. "I'll even quit the Cubs, so I'll have time."

I couldn't pass up an offer like that. So Irene found a teacher who gave split lessons in violin and piano (for the price of one), and Steve quit the Cub Scouts and knuckled down to the grind of learning two instruments.

For about two weeks it seemed as if it might work. Steve came right home after school, and instead of playing outside with his friends he went straight to his instruments and started practicing.

But after the rainy season was over, he showed his true colors. Soon his piano playing consisted of striking a few single notes so he could tune his violin, and his violin playing consisted of tuning up.

After a month of this, I'd had enough.

"See here," I said to Steve firmly. "I don't think you have the

164

time to split up your interests. You'll have to decide what you want to play and stick to it. Now make up your mind. What kind of lessons do you want to take?"

Steve looked at me with a completely straight face, and said, "I want to take tennis lessons!"

That ended Steve's formal education in music. If he wants to entertain at parties when he grows up, he can play "Up the Hill and Down the Hill" on the strings of his tennis racket.

14

Princeton: 6—*Everybody Loves Me:* 0

If there's any moral to this tale, it is: don't let your wife go to college. Keep her home where she belongs, folding diapers or wrangling with the washing-machine repairman. If she's still bored, let her do her own repair work on the washing machine. But by all means keep her home. Otherwise what happened to me might happen to you.

We were having a quiet evening at home the night Irene sprang it on me. And we were at the dinner table, which was still slightly damp from the glass of milk Andy had spilled just before he and Steve had slipped away to their room to look at television.

"You know what I'd like to do, dear?" said Irene, with a wistful expression. "I'd like to go back to college."

"And what's to become of me and the children?" I asked, suddenly visualizing our entire smooth-running household falling apart at the seams while she was off on some college campus pursuing a sheepskin. "Who'll sew our buttons on? Who'll do the cooking?"

"Don't be silly," Irene scolded me. "I don't mean regular college. I just want to take a course at UCLA extension two nights a week, from seven-thirty until ten."

"And what am I supposed to be doing those two evenings a week?" I asked.

"Oh, you and Mannie can do something together. Martha said she'd like to take the course with me."

Irene was talking about Martha and Mannie Manheim, our closest friends. We'd known them ever since Mannie had given me my first job as a writer on the Milton Berle radio show in 1942, and now they were neighbors of ours in Pacific Palisades.

"Okay, take the course," I said. "But just don't join a sorority. I don't believe in them."

The Manheims came to dinner on the evening the girls were to attend their first class. After Irene and Martha had departed for UCLA, Mannie and I sat down in the living room and contemplated each other sadly.

Mannie looks more like the owner of a successful string of furniture stores than he does a comedy writer. He's in his early fifties, with hair that is quite gray around the temples, bright eyes and a slightly plumpish figure that seems more at home in a business suit than sports apparel.

"Well, what'll we do?" Mannie finally asked, studying me as though he wished I were his pretty wife.

I shrugged. "Too bad neither of us likes to play cards."

"Or look at television."

"We could read poetry to each other," I suggested.

He ignored my attempt at levity. He was busy lighting a cigar. After savoring the first puff, he said simply, "Why don't we write a play?"

"I don't have any ideas for a play," I replied.

"Neither do I, but we could get one," he said, glancing at the clock. "It looks as if we're going to have plenty of time on our hands."

"I'm game," I said, "if you'll do the typing."

That was January, 1956. By February we had an idea. By March we had read all the books on how to write a play that we could find in the Santa Monica Public Library. And by mid-July we had completed a first draft of a three-act comedy called *Everybody Loves Me*, the story of an egomaniac television star's relationship with his son, his mistress and his business associates, and how he gets his comeuppance.

Since our wives were no longer attending class, we put them to work typing the play. When it was typed and all neatly bound in a flashy red manuscript cover, Mannie said, "Well, it looks like a play from the outside. Now what do we do with it? Know any stage producers?"

"I've known Max Gordon since I was a kid," I said. "He once told me he'd like to read my first play—if I ever wrote one."

"Why don't we send it to him?" suggested Mannie.

"Do you think it's good enough?"

"How'll we know unless we let someone read it?" he said, with a shrug. "At least we'll get a professional opinion."

Yes, we'll certainly get that, I thought as I dropped the large envelope containing our manuscript off at the post office that afternoon. If there was one thing Max Gordon was noted for, besides having produced a great many stage successes, it was his utter frankness. I shuddered as I thought of what he might say about our effort.

On Sunday afternoon—I mailed the manuscript on Thursday— the phone rang and the operator said New York was calling.

"Arthur," said an excitable voice I recognized as belonging to Max Gordon. "I'm going to produce your play on Broadway this fall."

"You are?" I exclaimed, taken aback. "How come?"

"Because I like it and think it's a fine play," he shouted enthusiastically. "Why in hell else do you think I'd want to produce it?"

"Pardon me," I said, putting my hand over the mouthpiece and relaying the news to Irene, who was a few feet away in the kitchen, making peanut-butter-and-jelly sandwiches for the children's lunch.

"I may faint!" gasped Irene.

"Irene may faint," I said into the phone.

"What in hell's the matter with you people out on the West Coast?" Gordon yelled at me. "Here I phone to tell you I'm going to produce your play, and you're acting like children."

"It's just that we're excited," I stammered. "It's our first play."

"Well, stop being excited and listen to me," Max continued

shouting. "We have to work fast if we're going to get this play on this fall—it's pretty late in the season already. Now, I want you and Mannie to get busy and make the final scene in the third act a little stronger. That's all the play needs—a little more work in the third act and some stronger curtain lines. But I can assure you that right now this play is closer to the finished product than any play I've ever had submitted to me."

The Marxes and the Manheims had a real celebration that night. Ordinarily we're pretty conservative drinkers, but this was one time we really let ourselves go. I had a Bourbon on the rocks, Mannie had a Scotch and water, Martha had a thimbleful of sherry and Irene had a No-Cal ginger ale.

But if we thought our work was finished, and that all we had to do was to sit back and wait for our royalties to start rolling in, we obviously didn't know the theater.

Oh, we realized there'd be some minor revisions. Gordon had already prepared us for that in my first conversation with him. But we were more than a little aghast at the number of major changes he suddenly started demanding in subsequent phone conversations.

"I don't understand this," Mannie finally told him. "I thought you liked our play. Now you want the whole thing changed."

"I *do* like it," replied Gordon. "I think it's great. So does Oscar Hammerstein. He read it last night. But remember one thing, boys—plays aren't written, they're *rewritten!* Now I want you to to get together with Bob Sinclair as soon as possible. And you listen to him. He knows."

Bob Sinclair was the man Gordon had signed to stage our play. Mannie and I had never heard of him, but he had a number of important stage hits to his credit, nevertheless—*Dodsworth, Pride and Prejudice, The Women, Babes in Arms* and *The Philadelphia Story.* He hadn't had any hits in recent years—in fact, he had turned to writing mystery stories and was leading the life of a country gentleman in Santa Barbara when he accepted our assignment—but Max assured us he was "still a fine director," so we took his word for it.

Sinclair turned out to be a dour-faced man in his mid-fifties, with a bushy head of gray hair, a quiet voice, and a habit of frequently dropping a lot of first names like Ronnie and Bonita, Oscar and Dick, Moss and George, and Gadge and Josh. He also had an attitude toward us and our play that was faintly alarming.

In our first meeting, Sinclair made it quickly known that as playwrights we had much to learn. As for the play itself, although it had the basic ingredients of a hit, he said it required a complete job of reconstruction, starting from page one. Again we said that we didn't see the point of making such drastic changes. After all, it was our original draft that had appealed to Max when he first read the play. But Sinclair simply smiled wisely, and said, "Plays aren't written, boys, they're rewritten."

We didn't know whether we agreed with this theory, but we certainly didn't want to be out of step with the times. We decided we'd better comply. "After all, we wouldn't want Sinclair to fire us," said Mannie.

However, before we could begin rewriting, we had to have a conference with Jack Carson, whom Max had signed, on our recommendation, to play the leading role of Gordy.

When he first read our play, Carson had been ecstatic in his praise of it. This was the stage vehicle he'd been waiting for all his life. His only concern was whether "I'll be good enough to do the part justice." But by the time we got together with him, he, too, had found a number of things he wanted changed, including the elimination of two of our favorite characters.

This time Mannie and I really put our foot down. We said that we, the authors, felt we knew better than anyone what should be in the play and what shouldn't. And since our original version was what had sold Max on the play in the first place, we felt we ought to stick with that.

"Well, if you just want to be stubborn and have a flop," said Sinclair, "that's your affair."

Having put our foot down, Mannie and I then went home and spent the next four weeks making the revisions that everyone had requested. By then we hardly recognized our original play. And our wives and children hardly recognized us; we'd been locked up in a room with a typewriter every day from nine in the morning until well past midnight, and they had almost forgotten what we looked like.

Max Gordon, in the meantime, had been on the long-distance phone nearly every day, pressuring us to complete the revisions. He wanted to go into rehearsal no later than the fifteenth of October.

Gordon would phone us from wherever he happened to be—his office, the steam room at the City Athletic Club, the baths at Saratoga Springs, or a hotel in Atlantic City where he had gone to rest up from the excitement of doing a new play.

From these various calls we learned:

(1) Max had let a number of people read our play and they all were of the unanimous opinion that we had a sure hit on our hands.

(2) Quite a few important people were investing in it, including Rodgers and Hammerstein, and the late Harry Cohn, who was then the head of Columbia Pictures.

(3) So many other people wanted to invest in it that Max couldn't accommodate all of them.

(4) He had booked our road tour (Princeton, Washington and Philadelphia).

(5) The Shuberts had given him their word that we could have a New York theater late in November.

(6) He was considering hiring a girl for the lead whose name was Temple Texas.

Miss Texas was virtually an unknown, Gordon revealed, but she was no amateur. She had played a featured role in *Pipe Dream*, and she had been highly recommended to Gordon by Oscar Hammerstein himself.

Gordon was willing to recognize our authors' prerogative to approve of any members of the cast before they were signed, if we insisted, but he urged us to make this one exception and take her sight unseen because she was so perfect for the part of Violet.

"If we don't sign her now," he warned us, "we're liable to lose her to the Judy Holliday show."

"Have you heard her read?" we asked.

"No, but I don't have to. I can tell she's going to be great just by looking at her. She's a lovely girl. And I have Oscar's word for it, too. So think it over, boys, and let me know your decision. And don't take too long."

While we were thinking it over the following day, we received a letter from Gordon informing us that he had just signed Temple Texas, and that he was extremely happy about it, as he knew we would be.

When the revisions were finished, we had the play mimeographed and shipped it off to Max Gordon.

Gordon phoned us from the steam room of the City Athletic Club on the following Sunday to tell us that he had just finished reading the revised version (how a myopic man with eyeglasses can do any reading in a steam room I never have figured out), and that he liked it very much. All but the finish, which he felt was too downbeat, even though it was a more honest ending. "But you can fix that when you're in New York," he added. "We're going into rehearsal the fifteenth of October for sure, so I want you and Mannie here no later than the twentieth of September."

I could hardly wait to go to New York and see our play in rehearsal (especially since I'd also be able to see the World Series). Irene was just as anxious to accompany me, but there were two things deterring us—Steve and Andy. And our favorite baby sitter, Irene's mother, had picked this unpropitious time to be off on one of those thirty-nine-day cruises to the Orient.

After much deliberation, Irene and I reached a decision. We explained to the children that:

(1) Daddy was going to go to New York by himself to help Mannie Manheim put on the play. ("No, dear, Daddy won't forget to send back some toys from F.A.O. Schwarz's.")

(2) Mommy would remain in California and take care of

Steve and Andy and the washing machine until Nanny
Grace returned from the Orient.

(3) As soon as Grace arrived, Mommy and Martha would join
Daddy and Mannie Manheim in New York.

(4) Mommy and Daddy would bring Steve and Andy on for
the New York opening—provided the public's clamor for
seats wasn't so overwhelming that there'd be nothing left
for the authors' children but standing room.

Though it was a blow to Steve and Andy that they couldn't go
on the plane with me to New York, they accepted our separation
stoically. And at the airport, they wished me godspeed and said
they hoped the plane would arrive in New York before F.A.O.
Schwarz closed for the day.

Mannie Manheim and I arrived in New York that evening, and
checked into a hotel in midtown Manhattan, near Steinway Hall.
It was a residential hotel that was filled with widows and elderly
couples who were spending their declining years there, playing
canasta and surreptitiously cooking meals on hot plates. But
except for the cooking odors in the corridors and the discordant
screaming of uncertain sopranos trying to hit high C in the neigh-
boring building, it was a comfortable place to live. And the rates
weren't too high as New York hotels go.

We had to consider that. Max Gordon might have been
paying our expenses, but our contract with him didn't stipulate
to what extent. Besides, we didn't want to be unfair. To make it
even easier on Gordon's pocketbook, Mannie and I had decided
to share a living-room—bedroom suite until our wives came on.

Mannie proved to be an ideal roommate—for a polar bear. He
insisted on having all the windows wide open. Not only did he
have a fondness for drafts, but when I was ready for bed that
night he refused to turn out the lights.

"Mind if I read a little?" he asked, dropping a large bundle
of newspapers on his bed.

It was then he confessed to me that he has insommia. He has

to drug himself into oblivion every night by reading the early editions of all the daily papers. Not only wouldn't he turn out the lights until he had devoured every bit of inconsequential news in the *Times, Tribune, News* and *Mirror*, but if he came across an interesting item in a gossip column he read it aloud to me.

"Did you see what it says in Hy Gardner's column?" he asked.

"How could I see it? I'm supposed to be sleeping."

"He says there are going to be a hundred shows trying out on the road this coming theatrical season, but there are only twenty-five available theaters in New York that they can come into. That sounds serious. I hope we can get one."

After hearing such reassuring news as that at three in the morning, I, too, had trouble getting to sleep. But at least I had the pleasure of knowing I could sleep late in the morning. That was one good thing about working in the theater. Nobody expected you to be up before noon.

We were awakened at 7:30 by the jangling of the telephone bell. Since we had left strict orders with the telephone operator that we didn't care to accept any calls until 9:30, I assumed, as I reached for the phone, that only an emergency, like the hotel being on fire from one of those hot plates, would cause her to disregard my orders. I was sure of it when the voice on the other end barked out, "This is the management!"

"Yeah, yeah. What's wrong?" I asked anxiously.

"Nothing's wrong," said the voice I still didn't recognize because I was only half-awake. "This is the management—Max Gordon—your producer! Have you got the new finish for the third act yet? I think the curtain should definitely come down with Gordy playing gin with Pinky. That's the finish Oscar likes."

"Max, we haven't written it yet," I said sleepily. "You told us we could work on that when we were in New York."

"For God's sakes! You've been here since last night. What the hell have you been doing with yourselves?"

"Ask him if he's got a theater yet," Mannie said to me.

I relayed his question to Max, who snapped back at me with, "Just leave the theater up to me, will you, boys? That's one thing

I never worry about. I never heard of a show yet that couldn't come into New York if it was any good. You just worry about the jokes—and getting a new third-act curtain. I'll get us a theater. Remember—this is a high-class management you're working for. I'm not one of those new young fellows who's suddenly decided he's a producer. I've had more hits than anybody on Broadway— *Roberta, Cat and the Fiddle, Band Wagon, Junior Miss, Dodsworth, Pride and Prejudice, The Women, Sister Eileen, Born Yesterday, Solid Gold Cadillac.* We didn't play any of those out in the street, you know. You just worry about the jokes. I'll worry about the theater."

Before Max could tell me about any more of his past successes, I made an appointment for Mannie and me to see him in his office at ten-thirty, and as quickly and diplomatically as possible ended our conversation.

When we arrived in Gordon's office, which was in an old building on the corner of Sixth Avenue and Forty-second Street, the reception room was crammed to capacity with actors, actresses and agents, all of whom had heard that Max was casting a new play. Not knowing who we were, Joe Olney, Gordon's stage manager, was about to shunt Mannie and me back to the end of the line, which by then extended into the outside corridor, when Max spied us and came rushing over excitedly with arms outstretched.

"Joe, these are my authors," he cried out. "Arthur and Mannie! Don't kick them out. We need them for the jokes. Come in, boys, come into my office."

After we were settled on the only available piece of furniture in the uncomfortably small office—a worn-out leather couch with protruding springs—Max sat down at his desk and put his feet upon it.

Max hadn't changed much in appearance since I had last seen him—in fact, since I had first seen him thirty years ago. His short, stocky figure was perhaps a little plumper, and his hair was slightly thinner and grayer. But he seemed just as robust and sharp-eyed and full of nervous energy as ever; and he was still wearing old-fashioned steel-rimmed spectacles, which, along with his roundish face and beaklike nose, gave him a somewhat owlish appearance.

"Tell me, boys," he said, with a warm smile. "How does it feel to be playwrights?"

"Wonderful," we said in unison.

"You know how long I've been in the show business, boys?" said Max. "Nearly fifty years. I've produced more hits than anybody on Broadway. I've given many famous playwrights their first chance. Actors and actresses, too. Judy Holliday, for instance. Why, I even produced one of Noel Coward's first plays in this country— *Design for Living*. We were always great friends after that. I'll never forget the time I invited him to come on the road with me to see a show of mine I was trying out. After the final curtain, he came running up the aisle to where I was standing, threw his arms around me ecstatically, and said, 'Max, dahling, it stinks!' " Max shook his head in wonderment. "It's a fascinating business, the legitimate theater. A guy like me couldn't be happy in any other medium. That's because I don't have to answer to anybody else. I can do what I like. That's why I bought your play. I liked it personally. I knew it was a fine play the minute I read it, because it has a great central character—that fellow Gordy. That's what I go by. And the story's good, too."

"We hope so," I said, "because we'd like to write more plays."

"You're smart," said Gordon. "The theater's the only place where a writer doesn't have to take orders. By the way, did you take that Italian with the fur coat out of the third act yet, like I told you to?"

I wasn't sure, but I imagined he was referring to the character of Palazzio, the furrier.

"We're not sure we want to take him out," I said.

"For God's sakes, boys, be reasonable!" exclaimed Gordon. "You can't have an Italian with a fur coat come on at twenty minutes to eleven. I tell you, you've *got* to take him out."

"We'll think about it," said Mannie. "Now how much expense money are you going to give us?"

Gordon appeared surprised. "You don't think *I'm* supposed to pay for you while you're in New York? I never paid an author's expenses in my life!"

"The contract says you're supposed to pay our fares to and from New York, if we're nonresidents, and all reasonable hotel and living expenses."

"Never heard of such a thing," snapped Gordon. He yelled for Al Golden, his bookkeeper and company manager, to come in. "Al," he said, as a heavy-set man with bushy black eyebrows and a waxen complexion entered the office, "the boys claim I'm supposed to pay their expenses. Is that right?"

Golden shrugged, and there was an uncomfortable moment while he found the disputed clause in the contract and read it aloud to Gordon, who listened sober-faced. When the reading was over, he said, "Okay, I guess I have to pay them, Al. Fix them up with some kind of a per diem allowance."

"I think the Guild stipulates fifteen bucks a day," said Golden, leaving.

Gordon said, "It's a good thing you boys got yourself a producer with a big bankroll." He laughed sardonically, and added, "It's no wonder it costs so much to put on a play these days. That's the trouble with show business. High expenses are killing it off. You used to be able to produce a one-set play like yours for ten thousand dollars. Now it costs seventy-five thousand."

"When do we meet Temple Texas?" asked Mannie.

"Two o'clock," said Gordon. "I tried to get her here this morning, but she was washing her hair." He pulled a watch chain from his vest—probably the last vest in New York—and, after noting the time, hurriedly stood up and put on his hat. "I have to get over to the club and take a dip in the tank. You boys can eat lunch with Sinclair. He ought to be here any minute."

As Max was leaving, Sinclair, who'd been in New York a week prior to our arrival, showed up with the bloom of a bad night's sleep still on his half-closed eyelids. After impressing us with how many actors and actresses he had interviewed since his arrival in the big city, he invited Mannie and me to be his guest at Sardi's.

At Sardi's, there was the usual jam-up of people without reservations in the entrance, hoping that fortune would smile on them and get them a table. Sinclair didn't have a reservation, either, but he confidently pushed his way through to the front of the crowd and waved to the headwaiter. But nobody recognized him. Finally, he managed to attract Vince Sardi's attention, and he explained who he was.

"Oh, yes, Robert Sinclair," said Sardi, with a faint glimmer of recognition in his eyes. "How are you? What are you doing these days? Been keeping busy?"

"I'm doing the Jack Carson show for Max Gordon," explained Sinclair. "Zolotow had a long story about it in the *Times*. We'll need a table every day until we go on the road."

Sardi glanced down his list of names and shrugged helplessly. "I have nothing downstairs for you right now. How about upstairs?"

I gathered, from the injured look on Sinclair's face, that to him there could be no greater proof of man's inhumanity to man than Sardi's suggestion that we dine upstairs. However, since the food is the same on both levels, and Mannie and I were both insisting that we were hungry and didn't care where we ate, Sinclair reluctantly agreed to a table in the steerage compartment.

During lunch, Sinclair said he had spent the weekend at Dorothy and Dick's (Rodgers, we presumed) country house. "Dick has a hell of a good notion what the finish of the play should be," he said.

He told us the proposed new ending, and we agreed to see if we could work it out. By then it was two o'clock, and we had to rush back to Gordon's office to meet our leading lady, Temple Texas.

Temple was a tall, attractive, statuesque blond of about thirty, whom, Mannie confessed to me in an aside, he wouldn't object to meeting in a wrestling match. She was dressed beautifully in a green suit, topped off with an expensive mink stole, and she was sporting a couple of dazzlingly large diamond rings. I had never seen so many carats before outside of a vegetable market.

"Max let me read the new version of your play," said Temple, in a barely noticeable Southern drawl. "Gee, you've given me some funny lines. It's a great part."

"You ought to be just right for it, too," Mannie assured her.

"I'm relieved," she smiled tensely. "I was afraid that maybe you wouldn't be as enthusiastic about me as Max was. Well, if that's all, I'd better be getting back uptown. I'm an interior decorator when I'm not working in a play, and I have an apartment I'm just finishing up."

Mannie and I wrote the new ending in a couple of days, and took it to Max. He read it in his own office while Sinclair, Mannie and I were in the adjacent cubicle, listening to an actor try out for one of the parts. Suddenly the door flew open and Max stuck his head in. "It's just wonderful, boys. It's so good I had to call up Oscar and read it to him over the phone. He thinks it's just right, too. Now if the public'll just go for this big guy Carson in the part—and you'll take that goddamned Italian out—we're in for a tremendous smash."

This big guy Carson, as Max persisted in calling our star, slipped into New York during the final week of casting, without the fanfare that usually accompanies the arrival of an important actor from Hollywood. That is to say, he didn't appear as the mystery guest on *What's My Line?* or even as a substitute panelist.

Mannie and I got our first glimpse of him in New York on the sidewalk outside the Forty-sixth Street Theater, where the big brains of the *Everybody Loves Me* company were congregating one noon to decide the fate of some more aspiring actors. (The auditions were to be held inside the theater, not on the sidewalk. We were just meeting outside the theater.)

Sinclair and Gordon were nowhere in sight when Mannie and I alighted from our cab, but Jack Carson, in dark glasses and a gray business suit with very wide lapels and shoulders, was already there, pacing nervously up and down the sidewalk under the marquee.

Although I had met Carson several times previously, I never failed to be surprised at what a giant of a man he was. He towered over us when we shook hands, and he seemed more like a retired football player than an actor.

"I guess I'm a little early," said Carson. "I'll never learn how to time those crosstown taxis. I've rented an apartment over on Sutton Place. MCA got it for me. I took it for a whole year."

"You must have a lot of confidence in the play," said Mannie.

"I have. I think it's got a great chance—if we don't mess it up in the casting. How's this doll Texas Temple, or Temple Texas, or whatever the hell her name is? She any good?"

"She looks good," I said. "I'm sure you'll like her."

"What kind of a name is Temple Texas? Sounds like a strip teaser."

"Her real name's Dora Temple. She comes from Texarkana."

"I just hope she's a pro," said Carson. "Amateurs make me nervous."

"Well, if she doesn't work out, you can always use Lola," said Mannie. "I saw her on the Skelton show. She's damn good."

"Don't even joke about a thing like that," said Carson. "Lola's a good little actress, but I don't think husbands and wives should work together. So do me a favor—don't even mention it kiddingly when Lola gets to town."

When the others still hadn't arrived by noon, Carson looked at his watch and said, "I could use a belt. Can I buy you one?"

At first I thought he was referring to something to hold up his pants, but when he steered us into Dinty Moore's a few doors away, and up to the bar, I realized he was not talking about haberdashery. Mannie and I accepted his offer to have a drink with him, and while we stood at the bar he said, "Boy, I sure had a night last night."

"When's Lola getting here?" asked Mannie nervously.

"Probably not for a couple of weeks yet. She's got some TV commitments on the Coast." He suddenly seemed downcast. "I'm on the loose until then. But I sure don't like it. I get lonely."

When we returned to the theater, Max was there, and he had

Temple Texas with him. "I thought you'd like to meet your lead-ing lady," he explained to Carson as he herded us through the stage entrance, across the dimly lit stage and down into the orchestra. "I want to see how you two look together. Would you mind standing next to Temple up on the stage, Jack?"

Carson didn't mind a bit. After he had stood with her long enough for us to see that they made a very striking pair, he and Temple read a scene together. The parts seemed to be made for them. We were delighted. So was Carson. He invited Temple to have a belt with him after the auditions were over. "Can't, Jack. I have to meet my boy friend." She laughed. "And I have to run right now. Good-by, everyone."

"Lovely girl," said Max, after Temple had departed. "You two ought to make a great team."

"She drops her t's and r's," said Carson. "I hope the audience can understand her."

While we were waiting for the first actor to audition, Max leaned back contentedly in his seat in the first row and said, "You know how many years I've been doing this? Forty years, and I still get a big thrill out of it."

He may have been thrilled, but after about fifteen minutes of auditions, we noticed that Max was taking little cat naps during the performances he didn't like. He even snored quite vociferously.

Carson was—and understandably—a little disturbed by his pro-ducer's apparent lack of interest in the proceedings. But Mannie and I told him not to worry. We'd been through a week of auditions already, and we now realized that this was Max's way of judging a performance. In order to qualify for a job, an actor or actress first had to be able to keep Max awake—even after lunch. He never fell asleep on a good actor—only the incompetents, which, to my mind, is as accurate a way to select performers as any I know.

Eventually enough actors came along who managed to keep Max awake, and by the Friday morning before we were to go into rehearsal we had rounded up a cast with which everyone was satisfied, and Max had signed all but one of them to contracts.

That one was Conrad Janis, whom we wanted for the very important role of Jack Carson's twenty-two-year-old son.

We had auditioned him only that morning, and all of us had been tremendously impressed by his acting and looks. Max had not only stayed awake, but he had jumped out of his seat halfway through the audition and rushed back to his office to phone Conrad Janis' agent.

However, by the time Mannie and I returned to the office Max's jubilation had disappeared and he was sitting forlornly at his desk, with his hat still on. "I couldn't get him," he groaned. "His agent wants five hundred a week. Imagine, boys, five hundred a week for a young pup like that. It's outrageous. No wonder I've had four nervous breakdowns."

"But Max," I pleaded, "five hundred a week isn't too much these days for a good actor. He can make that much on T.V. any time he wants."

"That's the trouble with the show business these days," said Gordon. "It's spoiling all the young actors. All they want to do is make money. Well, I can't pay those fancy prices in a legit show. It runs our nut too high."

"Why don't you phone him back and offer him three hundred?" suggested Mannie.

"If he wants the part bad enough, he'll phone me."

He'd barely got the words out of his mouth when the phone rang. It was Conrad's agent. "I'll give him two fifty and not a penny more," barked Gordon.

After the agent had accepted his offer, Max leaned back in his worn-out chair, lighted a long cigar, and said rather jubilantly, "Why pay more when you can pay less?"

Rehearsals were set for the following Monday morning, at the Booth Theater, on the corner of Forty-fifth Street and Shubert Alley. Irene and Martha had arrived on Saturday, and were eager to attend the first rehearsal with us. But when we mentioned this to Sinclair, he said, "I'd rather you didn't bring your wives, boys.

The first few days I just want you and Max and the cast. Strangers might make the actors nervous."

"Strangers, indeed!" pouted Martha, when the four of us were sitting around late Saturday night, hashing the thing over. "If it weren't for us, there wouldn't even be a play!"

"I don't think we have anything to complain about," I said. "Feuer and Martin don't even let the *authors* in the theater."

When Mannie and I arrived backstage at the Booth Monday morning, we were surprised to see how many new additions there were to the "cast." The script, the last time we had glanced at it, had contained only eleven parts. But there were considerably more than eleven people milling around the stage on this particular morning. There were in addition to the cast: Nat Dorfman, the publicity man, and his wife, son and daughter-in-law; Frank Stempel, Carson's manager; Joe Carter, Carson's valet; Bob Alda, a close friend of Carson's; Al Golden; a photographer and his assistant; a Yorkshire terrier who belonged to Temple Texas; the fountain boy from the Astor drugstore who had come over with coffee and doughnuts for one of the actors and who had decided to stick around and see how the show looked to him; and a number of unidentified men and women who presumably were friends and relatives of the actors.

There was even on hand an unemployed friend of Joe Olney, our stage manager. He was an Italian character actor, who was still hopeful of getting the part of Palazzio, even though he'd been told it was no longer in the play.

Yes, Max Gordon had finally convinced us that we didn't need the fur-coat bit. He hadn't exactly convinced us. He had simply refused to hire an actor for the part, so there was nothing we could do but bow to his judgment.

Rehearsals were conducted on a bare stage, illuminated by a single 1,000-watt light bulb that hung suspended from the flies and blinded anyone who looked in that general direction.

The first reading was done with the actors sitting around in straight-backed chairs in a large semicircle, like a minstrel show. It sounded surprisingly good, in spite of the fact that most of the cast, including Temple and Carson, were working under the handicap of having bad head colds. While actors and actresses were struggling with unfamiliar lines, you could hear paroxysms of coughing in the background and the rustling of Kleenex boxes. (The next day, at rehearsal, Max brought in a doctor and bludgeoned even those who didn't want them into taking cold shots.)

Colds and all, however, it was a very encouraging first reading. The actors were laughing it up at all the lines—even the straight ones—in order to show the authors how grateful they were for the privilege of being in such a fine play. The authors were laughing it up in order to show the actors that they were appreciated, even though they were mangling some of their favorite lines. The director was laughing it up in order to show the female members of the company that he wasn't always all business. Joe Olney's Italian friend was laughing it up in hopes that if he showed himself to be a good enough fellow someone might feel sorry for him and put back the fur-coat scene. And the producer was laughing loudest of all—to prove to himself what a great judge of material he was.

When the reading was over, Max applauded and exclaimed, "In all my years in the show business, I've never heard a finer rendition of a play on the opening day of rehearsal. This guy Carson is great! And so is the rest of the cast. I tell you, boys, we've got a hit, unless I'm crazy."

One actor was so overcome with emotion that he even offered to buy into the play, if Max would let him, which he wouldn't.

By the second week of rehearsal most of this good feeling had disappeared and had been supplanted by little undercurrents of hostility and jealousy.

The actors, no longer in any real danger of being fired after surviving the five-day test period, were finding it quite within their province to demand of the authors that they give them more and funnier lines, and to complain to the director that "So-and-so is deliberately stepping on my laugh lines."

The authors, who had shown admirable restraint the first week, had now lost their initial bashfulness and were beginning to complain to the director that some of the things they were seeing and hearing on the stage were not exactly as they had originally conceived them.

The director was beginning to tell the authors that *he* knew more about how their lines should be read than they did.

The star was beginning to complain about his leading lady's lack of stage experience and her Texan drawl.

His leading lady was beginning to complain that she couldn't very well give a decent performance if the star persisted in throwing her the wrong cues, and making her self-conscious about the way she talked.

Joe Olney's Italian friend was predicting a flop if the fur-coat scene didn't go back in.

And the producer was beginning to holler at the authors for not eliminating certain lines that contained "damn" and "hell" from the script. "For Christ's sake," he used to say. "Do you want me to be embarrassed when all my friends see it?"

Aside from the internal frictions, there were important decisions to be made every day during rehearsals. For instance: where were we going to eat lunch?

Carson favored Dinty Moore's, because the portions were larger. Sinclair was always holding out for Sardi's, because he was afraid of losing his downstairs table if we didn't show up for it regularly. And Mannie and I, feeling the pinch of Max's per diem allowance and being the only ones in the company not on salary, felt that Nedick's was more within our budget.

Max had problems of another nature. The bangtails were running at Belmont Park, and Max, being an avid horseplayer, wanted to be out there to root home his losers. But this made it pretty difficult for him to keep up with the progress of the play, there being no place near the pari-mutuel windows where we could rehearse.

He finally settled for going to the track on just Wednesdays and Saturdays. On all other days he dropped into the Booth at regular intervals to supervise rehearsals and to keep us abreast of how he was doing in regard to getting us a theater for the New York opening.

Despite his bravado, Max wasn't having as much success with this as he had originally anticipated. He claimed he had been offered a number of theaters, but that *he* had turned them down because he was holding out for the best location. But he wasn't fooling any of us.

Finally, during the last week of rehearsals, Max told us he had made a deal for a theater. "We're getting the Belasco. We open there the twenty-second of December."

"Why so late in the season?" I inquired.

"Because I can't get one before then," he admitted angrily. "That's why."

"What'll we do until then?" asked Mannie.

"We'll stay on the road. We'll make a bundle, too, with this guy Carson in the lead. There's a lot of money in touring if you've got a star."

Nobody was overjoyed at the prospect of leading a gypsy life on the road for six weeks before Christmas, least of all Martha and Irene. But, as Mannie said, who asked them to go to college?

However, our dispositions improved considerably the end of that week, when Irwin Allen, a movie producer from one of the major studios, who had read our script, phoned us from Hollywood and said he'd like to buy our play for a picture. He hinted at a figure of about $100,000.

Since coming to New York, Mannie and I had read the death notices of about a dozen highly touted plays that had opened to bad reviews and closed within a couple of days. We hadn't lost faith in *Everybody Loves Me*, but we felt it might be wise to sell it to the movies while we had the opportunity.

But when we told Max, whose consent was also necessary, that we wanted to make a movie deal, he was quite upset.

First of all, he told us, he had a moral obligation to Columbia Pictures to give them first crack at the movie rights, since they had money in the play. And secondly, he didn't feel that $100,000 was very much money, when you considered that it had to be split between the producer and the writers. "As long as you've waited this long," the sage of Broadway advised us, "why don't you wait until after it opens? Then you can sell it for some *real* money. You know what we got for *Born Yesterday?* A million dollars!"

"Suppose it's a flop?" asked Mannie.

"Then you won't get a quarter for it," Gordon chuckled. "But look how sore at yourselves you'll be if you give it away for a hundred grand and it turns out to be a smash. That's how I feel."

"You can afford to gamble," said Mannie. "We can't."

"Okay," said Gordon, "but I won't let you sell it for a cent less than $250,000, plus a bonus sliding scale of $1,000 a week for every week it plays on Broadway. That's the only way we can protect ourselves, boys."

When the Hollywood producer was apprised of Gordon's terms, he was a little shocked and said he wasn't sure if he could persuade his studio bosses to sink that much money into a play that hadn't even opened yet. "Don't forget, they only paid a hundred grand for Auntie Mame. But I'll try my best," Irwin Allen assured us, "because I think it'll make a hell of a picture."

That conversation took place on Saturday. On Monday our whole company was to leave for three days of rehearsals at the McCarter Theater in Princeton, where we were to open on Thursday. If we were to make a pre-production deal, it would have to be done before then.

Sunday was our last day in New York, and I don't think I'll ever forget it.

Max had arranged for five hundred people to see a preview of the play that afternoon at the Booth Theater. The curtain was supposed to go up at two o'clock, but at five minutes of two, Jack Carson, blissfully unaware of the time, was still in bed in his apartment. A frantic phone call from the stage manager roused him out of his torpid state, and at two-thirty-five Carson arrived at the theater in a taxicab.

"For God's sakes, Carson, it's about time," Gordon shouted at him.

"Sorry, Uncle Max," said Carson, with a sheepish grin. "The switchboard girl forgot to wake me."

Gordon, Mannie and I stood in the rear of the theater during the performance and watched from there. We thought it would be safer that way. As Max so cheerfully put it when we were anxiously waiting for the curtain to go up, "We'd better be someplace where we can get out of here in a hurry. If this guy Carson can't remember his lines, the audience will be chasing us with sticks."

There is no worse time for an author of a comedy than when he is waiting for the audience's reaction to the first few lines of his play. It is then—and only then—that he can tell whether he's written a comedy or not.

If there's only a mild laugh, there's hope. If the line just lies there dead, you know it's going to be rough going the rest of the performance.

Mannie and I couldn't quite believe the reception the play got that afternoon. From the moment the curtain went up until it went down two hours later, the theater rocked with laughter. Some lines even drew applause. "We're in," Mannie whispered to me during one of the big comedy scenes.

And if we'd been worried about Jack Carson, we needn't have been. After getting off to a shaky start, he came through with one of the finest performances I have ever seen. What's more, the audience loved him. They laughed raucously at his comedy lines, and during the dramatic scenes in the third act, the audience sat so tensely quiet that you could almost hear the cogs in Max's head mentally calculating how much money he was going to make from this venture.

After a line that got a particularly big laugh, Max would rush over to Mannie and me, pound us excitedly on the chest with both fists, and exclaim, "This is the biggest thrill I've ever had. In all my years in the theater—*Roberta, Dodsworth, Band Wagon, Sister Eileen, Cadillac*—I've never seen a preview go like this."

At the final curtain a cheer went up that could only have been duplicated at the opening of *My Fair Lady*. Carson took nine curtain calls.

Max threw his arms around Mannie and me, and said, "Well, I'll tell you one thing, boys. There's not going to be any pre-production movie deals now. We're going to wait until we open and sell this thing for a million dollars! I won't let you sell it for a cent less. You'll be thanking me six months from now."

With the preview crowd's applause still ringing pleasantly in our ears, Mannie and I and our wives were supremely confident as we traveled to Princeton Monday morning with the rest of the cast in a privately chartered Greyhound bus. We foresaw a very rosy future, marred only by the regular visits of the income-tax collector coming to get his rightful share of the million dollars. Irene was even considering sending her mother's mink coat, which she had borrowed for the trip, back to California and buying one of her own.

We were in even better spirits when we arrived in Princeton and saw that it was jampacked and jumping with out-of-town visitors. Evidently there was more interest in the opening of *Everybody Loves Me* than we had thought there would be.

But, as we learned when we were checking into the Princeton Inn, the influx of old grads and their wives and assorted friends and relatives of the student body had nothing to do with us. They were in town for that weekend's Harvard-Princeton football game; and from what we were able to gather from Al Golden, they were evincing not the slightest interest in contributing to the financial well-being of the *Everybody Loves Me* company. And neither were the native Princetonians.

Since the tickets to our show had gone on sale, we had taken in a grand total of $800. (The show that had preceded us, *The Sleeping Prince*, had grossed $13,000 for the same three-day stand.)

"I can't understand this," Max bleated to us in the privacy of his hotel suite. "We're not drawing a quarter at the box office. We're going to lose a fortune at this rate."

Mannie and I weren't as disturbed as I suppose we should have been. We felt that if the show went well opening night—and we had no reason to believe it wouldn't—the people who did see it would soon spread the word that *Everybody Loves Me* was something not to be missed, and that there would then be a wild scramble for tickets for the remaining performances.

Sinclair held the dress rehearsal Wednesday night, and if there was any truth to the show-business legend that a bad dress rehearsal means a successful opening, then we were in for the smash of all time. The actors, still not used to the set after three days of rehearsing in it, were tripping over stairs, bumping into furniture, losing props, forgetting where doors were, failing to remember lines, and adding some gems of their own.

All in all, you would have had to wait a long time to see a worse performance than the one to which we were treated Wednesday night. You would have had to wait until the following night—our opening.

We managed to have a full theater by the time the curtain went up. There were many New Yorkers there, including agents, friends and relatives of the actors, ticket brokers and the people who book theater parties. There was a frightfully small percentage of legitimate customers. And the other eight hundred people were in on passes issued by Max, who felt we ought to have a full house in order to get an accurate audience reaction.

We got one, but it wasn't good.

The play evidently needed a lot of work. It seemed overlong and full of lines that produced coughing instead of laughing. I wished I'd had the cough-drop concession that night. The performances were rough, too. Jack Carson didn't forget any lines, but he appeared nervous, and so did the rest of the cast. Their timing was all off, and everybody was stepping on everybody else's laughs—when there were any.

Strangely enough, *Variety*, the so-called "Bible of show business," gave the play a rave review the next day. It was such a rave that we were inundated with telegrams and long-distance calls from friends and relatives on the West Coast—all congratulating us on our victory.

Luckily for us, our friends back in civilization didn't see what the local critics had to say about our offering. They didn't like our play a bit, and they were quite vitriolic in saying so.

I thought the cast would be demoralized—I know Mannie and I were—but nobody else was terribly disturbed. The consensus seemed to be that these were just small-time reviewers, whose critical faculties had obviously been impaired by living in New Jersey too long.

"I heard they knifed *Bus Stop* here, too," said Carson, "and look what a hit that was in New York. These people just don't know."

It was the only sensible thing to do—blame it on the audience. You could always get a new audience (especially if you let them in the theater for nothing), but you couldn't write a whole new play between now and our Washington opening. We could strengthen it, by sharpening as many lines as we could, and cutting out the dead wood, but that was all we'd have time to do.

Max wasn't demoralized either—yet. "I'm not worried about the reviews," he said. "*Cadillac* got such bad reviews in Washington I was afraid to show them to George Kaufman. Still it was a hit by the time we brought it into New York. What worries me is the box office. We're going to drop eight grand this week. I never heard of a Max Gordon play doing such little business."

"Don't worry, Uncle Max," Jack Carson assured him. "I'm a big draw in Washington."

Carson may have been a big draw in Washington—but not in our play. When we checked into the National Theater in the capital, the manager informed us, in tones that were none too friendly, that we were going to have practically an empty house, unless Max gave away a lot of free seats.

A play of Arch Oboler's was opening the same night at a rival theater, and they had a Theater Guild subscription. We had trouble *giving* seats away.

We thought that our play, with the improvements we'd made in the last three days, went over slightly better in Washington than it had in Princeton. Several times the audience laughed, and Max's close friend, Supreme Court Justice Douglas, who was there as his guest, told us when it was over that he had had a very enjoyable evening. "Well, it's not drawing a quarter," Max barked at him. "Tell me, Justice, wouldn't you think *my* name would mean something in Washington?"

191

"Washington's always very quiet the week after a Presidential election," Douglas replied.

It wasn't as quiet as Irene and I were when we read the reviews the next morning. The first one started off with, "Nobody loves *Everybody Loves Me*." That was the kindest thing any of the critics had to say about us.

"Well, let's go sightseeing," I finally said. "I've always wanted to jump off the Washington Monument."

Shortly after breakfast—and a very cheap one, I might add— Max summoned Mannie, Sinclair and me to his suite in the hotel.

Max, wearing pajamas and a navy-blue bathrobe, was sprawled out on the Victorian chaise in the Victorian-furnished living room, with crumpled-up copies of the morning papers on the floor around him.

"Well, boys, it certainly don't look good," said Max encouragingly. "It certainly don't look good."

"Maybe we can fix it between now and Philadelphia," said Mannie.

"You can't fix those God-awful reviews," groaned Max.

"You told us *Cadillac* got panned here," I reminded him.

"Yes, but we had a Theater Guild subscription to keep us going while we worked on it. By the time we got to New York, it was okay. But we're losing a fortune, and those reviews are going to hurt the box office even more. Don't you understand? You can't keep on dropping ten grand every week. You soon go broke."

"Why don't you get Dorfman to do more publicity?" suggested Mannie.

"Publicity doesn't mean a thing," said Max. "They either want the play or they don't. And so far they don't."

Max sat there for a moment, staring numbly into space. Then, with the look of someone who wasn't licked yet, he suddenly strode to the desk, picked up the Sheraton-Carlton's quill pen and started writing very rapidly on a piece of hotel stationery. He didn't tell us what he was writing, but, judging by the intensity of his expression, I figured he was taking the bull by the horns and writing us a whole new play that the critics in the next town would go wild about.

When he finished writing, he said, "I just wrote Oscar Hammerstein a letter in Australia. How does it sound? 'Dear Oscar: I'm enclosing the Washington reviews. They are very bad. Evidently they don't want the play. We lost $8,000 in Princeton. I guess you and I made a mistake. Regards, Max.'" Max turned to Mannie. "Is it all right?" he asked.

"All right for what?" asked Mannie. "What's the point?"

"For God's sakes—I'm telling him what's going on. That's the point. Is it all right?"

"It's all right with me," shrugged Mannie, as bewildered as I by Max Gordon's behavior.

Since it was apparent that we weren't going to get any further constructive help from our producer, Mannie and I slunk out, saying we would try to fix some of the things in the play that the critics had picked on most vehemently.

Closeted in a smoke-filled hotel room, Mannie and I stuck to our typewriter all that week, while Carson and the rest of the cast, slightly demoralized by now but still hopeful that things would be better in Philadelphia, valiantly struggled to memorize the many new lines we were throwing at them between performances.

On Friday Max called us to his room and told us to stop writing. "I don't want the actors any more confused than they are. I want the performances to be as smooth as possible when we hit Philadelphia. That's going to be our last stand on the road, and the reviews had better be good. I've cancelled out Boston and Baltimore. With business the way it is, I can't afford to stay on the road six weeks. Before we left for Princeton, I had thirty-five grand to play with on the road. That should have been ample, even with moderate losses. But, Jesus, we can't drop what we're dropping."

"How can we go into New York early, without a theater?" asked Mannie.

"I don't know. Maybe we won't come in at all. I'll let you know after the reviews. If they're even fair, we've got a chance."

The outlook didn't seem very promising, in spite of the fact that

Carson told us, "Don't worry, boys. I'm a big draw in Philadelphia."

Philadelphia, Thanksgiving week, seemed an excellent reason for going South for the winter. It was cold, and the weatherman was forecasting a snowstorm. Still, there was something about the city that seemed friendlier than Washington. Perhaps it was the cheerful Thanksgiving decorations in the store windows. Or perhaps it was the fact that we'd sold out the first two performances of *Everybody Loves Me*.

Of course, there were still the critics to contend with, but Mannie and I had stopped worrying about what they would say. There are only a certain number of derogatory statements a critic can write about a play, and we believed that the Philadelphia critics would be hard pressed to think of anything we hadn't already read in Princeton and Washington.

So it was with little concern that the condemned authors and their wives, after a hearty last supper at their hotel, went to the opening Monday night at the Locust Theater. It was only when the laughs started rolling in, boisterously and frequently, that we felt our luck might be changing.

And it had. Both Philadelphia papers, the *Inquirer* and the *Bulletin*, came out in favor of *Everybody Loves Me* the next morning. They implied it might not be quite so good a play as *Hamlet*, but they said it was a fast and funny comedy, and it deserved the tremendous audience reaction it received.

It was like a last-minute reprieve. And when we were summoned to Max's room at eleven o'clock that morning, we were sure our producer would be in a celebrating mood.

Max was now in a room about the size of a closet. All the lights were on, and the place smelled of dead cigars. Max was lying on the bed, in undershorts and a bathrobe, looking rather like the last days of Camille. Al Golden was staring morosely out the airshaft, and Sinclair was flipping over the pages of a magazine.

"We're closing Saturday night!" said Max bluntly.

I was astounded. "I thought you said if the reviews were good—"

"They're not *money* reviews," Max cut me off sharply. "I just phoned the theater and there isn't a soul at the box office buying tickets for the rest of the week."

"What do you expect at eleven in the morning?" asked Mannie. "And it's snowing, besides."

"If those were money reviews, there'd be a line around the block already," said Max. "We can't even afford to finish out the two weeks here. I'll drop another ten grand this week alone. I'll be lucky if I can pay the cast's railroad fare back to New York."

"But you haven't given the reviews a chance to do any good," insisted Mannie. "Why don't you take out a newspaper ad and quote them?"

"What's the use of kidding ourselves, boys?" said Max. "The jig is up. I've given you a fine production, but you two don't seem able to fix what's wrong with the play, and the people just don't want it."

"They loved it last night," said Mannie. "Why don't you at least finish the two weeks here? Maybe it'll catch on."

"Supposing it does?" Max glowered at us. "Then where do we go? I don't have the money left to take a chance on Baltimore and Boston, and even if I did, I've lost the bookings. We can't have the Belasco until the twenty-second of December. What do you expect me to do—put it on in the middle of Times Square? There's no use arguing, boys. There's no place left but the warehouse." He took off his bathrobe and started pulling on his trousers. "Let's go over to the theater and tell the actors."

I'll never forget the scene in the theater, with the actors sitting around the dimly lighted and chilly stage, and Max, bundled up in his hat and overcoat, explaining the economic facts of show business to them. "It's too bad," he concluded. "If this were the old days, you could ask the actors and stagehands to take a cut while you stayed on the road long enough to get into shape. And *you'd* have been damn glad to co-operate. But today, with the unions and Equity and high expenses in general, there's nothing you can do when you get into trouble but close down."

It was a heartbreaking speech for Max to have to make, and he said it with such sincerity that for the first time I realized that it isn't so easy being the producer of a play, either—especially a flop. I felt genuinely sorry for him.

The announcement stunned the cast. Temple and Sue Randall, our ingénue, burst into tears. The men sat there in silence. Finally, one member of the cast—a middle-aged character actor—stood up and shouted, "I know who's really to blame." He pointed an accusing finger at Mannie and me. "It's those two! We've put seven weeks of our lives into this play of theirs, and what have they been doing? Writing new lines, when they should have been writing whole new scenes. It's criminal. Are we going to take it lying down?"

It sounded like the build-up to a scene in which the authors would be taken out and lynched. I started looking around for the nearest exit.

"You ought to be ashamed of yourself," Max yelled at the actor. "The boys did the best they could."

The others crowded around the indignant actor and demanded that he apologize to us. He refused. Somebody took a swing at him. He fell over backward into a chair, and a small brawl ensued, with all the men joining in.

"Don't bust up the furniture, boys!" Al Golden shouted at them. "We can still sell that."

While Golden was trying to break up the fight, Mannie and I sneaked out of the theater.

It was snowing hard when we reached the street. We walked along, neither of us saying anything for about a block. Then Mannie tapped me on the shoulder and said, "You know something, Marx? The next time the girls decide to go to college, I think we ought to go with them."

Gordon and Sinclair fled to New York that afternoon. But we couldn't get a plane out of Philadelphia for California until Thursday morning, which, ironically enough, was Thanksgiving.

When Irene and I were checking out of the hotel, the room clerk handed us a post card that he said had come in the day before. It was from our children, and this is what they wrote us:

DEAR MOMMY AND DADDY,
We hope you have a nice turkey for Thanksgiving.
Love,
STEVE AND ANDY

It was a huge turkey, and it cost $75,000.

15

Last Chapter

One of the drawbacks of writing a play is that all your friends know the exact degree of your success or failure. When you publish a book, nobody can be sure how many copies it sold. Unless you reveal them, the facts remain hidden in your publisher's royalty statement, which in turn lies buried in the dark recesses of your filing cabinet. But when you write a play that flops, your friends are instantly aware of it, for they've been following its progress in *Variety*. They might have missed the one good review *Variety* gave you, but you can be sure they'll see the obituary notice.

GORDON SHUTTERS "LOVES ME" IN PHILLY

Once they read a thing like this, you are automatically relegated to a lower rung on the Hollywood social ladder. In our case, we were bound to plummet from the B to the C Group—maybe even the D Group. After all, our show didn't even fold in New York.

I was aware of all this as Irene and I were winging our way westward in one of those flying cocktail lounges on Thanksgiving Day. And I felt pretty embarrassed about it, too. How would I ever be able to face our friends? I had left for New York in a blaze of glory, Max Gordon's fair-haired boy. I was returning the same schlepper of old.

However, I was more concerned about what Steve and Andy might think of me. I knew how anxiously they'd been looking forward to a trip to New York to see the opening on Broadway. Now that they had been euchred out of this adventure, they were bound to be pretty sore at me. They might even refuse to accompany their Grandmother Grace to the airport to meet us.

But as it turned out, they didn't hold the flop against us at all. When we alighted from the plane at International Airport at five o'clock (or *Mickey Mouse Club* time minus thirty), Steve and Andy were waiting at Gate 7 with Grace. Seeing us, they broke away from their grandmother's side, rushed up to Irene and me, and bombarded us with hugs and kisses, just as if we were coming home with a big hit.

"Sorry the show closed," said Steve, after the initial round of gee-you're-looking-wonderfuls was over and the five of us were walking to the car. "But I'm glad you're home sooner, anyway. Now we can all have Thanksgiving dinner together."

Andy, never one to wax sentimental for very long, said he was glad we were home, too, but added, at the first opportunity, "What did you bring us?"

"We have some surprises for you in our suitcase," smiled Irene. "But I'm afraid you'll have to wait until we get home so we can unpack them."

"Oh, boy!" cried out Andy. "Let's hurry up and go home so we can get our handy, economical, ready-to-use new toys." (The influence of television commercials on Andy's vernacular was becoming downright alarming.)

Grace was delighted to see us, too. And why not? We were the army of occupation coming to liberate her from six weeks of having to match wits with two of the most restless natives in Pacific Palisades.

"Gee, you two are looking marvelous," said Grace when we were driving home. "And Irene—I've never seen your hair so pretty. You must have found a marvelous place to get it done in Philadelphia."

"Oh, I did, only it wasn't in Philadelphia—we weren't there long enough. It was in Washington, at the Statler beauty shop. The girl who did it was named Gigi."

"Well, you ought to remember that place," said Grace.

"Yes, it'll come in handy in case she decides to run for Congress," I said.

"It's certainly great to be back in Southern California," said Irene, gazing wistfully out the car window at the beautiful row of stately telephone poles that bordered the highway (in the travel posters, they are palm trees). "I don't think I'll ever go away again. How's everything at the house, Mother?"

"Marvelous—marvelous," replied Grace. "Things have been running very smoothly. And these two boys of yours—they're just the best-behaved boys in the whole Pacific Palisades. Steve's been the regular little man of the house while you were gone. He's been sitting at the head of the table every night, and helping me lock up when it's time to go to bed. He's been an awfully big help."

"I've been an awful help, too," said Andy. "Harriet's been letting me feed the cat. And you know what? Sassy cats like Sassy Cat Food."

"Cat?!" I said, surprised. I knew who Harriet was. She was the housekeeper we had hired to help Grace take care of the house while we had been away. But I wasn't aware that we had put a cat on the payroll, too. "What cat?"

"Your new neighbors across the street had a whole litter," explained Grace.

"I didn't know a cat could afford to buy that house," I said.

"Their name is Harmon—their *cat* had a litter," said Grace. "And they offered to give Steve and Andy one. The children begged me to let them keep it, so I said it was all right. It's really very cute."

"I named him Tabby," said Steve. "Nanny lets him sleep in my room."

"You're sure it's a he?" asked Irene, worried.

"Pretty sure," answered Steve.

"When will you know definitely?" I asked.

"When he has kittens," replied Steve. "That's how the Harmons said we can tell definitely."

"Fine neighbors," I said.

"I hope he doesn't scratch up all the furniture," said Irene.

"He's really very well behaved," said Grace. "And he gets along wonderfully with Lucky, too."

"You'll like him," Steve assured us. "So we can keep him—can't we? Please, Mom?"

"If it's all right with your father," said Irene, winking at me.

"Sure we can keep him," I said. "I've always wanted a cat."

"You have?" said Steve.

"Certainly," I said. "I was telling your mother on the way home in the plane today—if there's one thing we need to make our life complete, it's a cat."

"Oh, boy!" exclaimed Andy. "You're sure nice. I think I'll give you a come-home present." He reached into his pocket and brought out a dusty, unwrapped piece of a chocolate candy bar that had a small bite nibbled off one end. "Have a delicious Mounds," he said, "made of rich dark chocolate and tree-ripened fresh coconut, for between-meal energy." (A further argument for pay T.V.)

When we arrived home, our household staff was waiting for us on the front steps, just as it's done in the English movies. Lined up to greet us were Harriet, Lucky (with a large scratch on her nose) and the new boarder, Tabby—a black-and-white cat of conglomerate lineage.

"Welcome home!" said Harriet, planting a kiss on my cheek. At the same time Lucky jumped up on me with her forepaws and the cat leaped on my shoulder and started licking my neck with his sandpaper tongue. "Everybody loves you here, anyway, Mr. Marx!" Harriet assured me.

After dislodging the cat from my shoulder—it took three people to pull him off—I started to get the bags out of the car.

"Let me help," offered Steve, picking up a suitcase.

"Me, too," said Andy, selecting a smaller one.

I was amazed at how grown-up they had become during our absence. And it was gratifying to see that they had acquired such a strong desire to be helpful.

"Now can we have our presents?" said Andy, dropping the suitcase he'd been carrying in the front hall and starting to fiddle with the latch. "Are the presents in this one?"

No matter what their motives were, they'd certainly been a help in carrying in the luggage. To reward them, we opened the suitcases, right there in the entrance hall, and divided up the spoils.

We hadn't been able to carry anything very large or exciting in our suitcases—mostly mementos of the trip: T-shirts with "Princeton" lettered on them; miniature Statues of Liberty from New York; pennants from Washington; tri-cornered hats from Mount Vernon; the Declaration of Independence from Independence Hall (not the original); and an old copy of an *Everybody Loves Me* program with Jack Carson's smiling picture on it (why he was still smiling I'll never know).

"These are good," said Andy, after taking stock of what he had received, but he seemed disappointed.

"Yeah, thanks a lot," said Steve. He seemed slightly disappointed, too.

"We couldn't carry the wind-up train and the erector set you wanted on the plane," explained Irene, guessing what was on their minds. "We'd have been overweight. We had them mailed. Gee, the house looks good to me."

"When will the toys get here?" asked Andy.

"Oh, probably the first of the week, darling."

"What day?" asked Steve.

"Something smells awfully good," I said, sniffing the air, which was heavy with the aroma of roasting turkey.

"Wait until you see the feast Harriet has prepared," said Grace. "She's been working on it for two days."

"And guess what, Daddy? We're having sweet potatoes, with delicious Campfire Marshmallows from the large economy box," explained Andy, smacking his lips. (Obviously, he had spent the entire six weeks we were away in front of the television set.)

"Dinner's ready!" announced Harriet gaily, throwing open the doors to the dining room. "Better come in while it's hot."

The dining table was festooned with Thanksgiving decorations. In the center was a huge horn of plenty filled with fruit and nuts, and in front of my place, on a carving board, was the

turkey, which looked delicious enough to make me forget the more horrible connotations of the word.

"This certainly looks great," I remarked, as I picked up the carving knife.

"It ought to," said Andy. "It's eviscerated—and for only a few cents more per pound!"

Toward the end of the meal, when the pumpkin pie had disappeared from our dessert plates, and we were sitting at the table in a pleasantly torpid state, sipping our coffee, the conversation once again veered back to *Everybody Loves Me*. Grace wanted to know everything that had happened, so we gave her a complete run-down of all the highlights and lowlights of our trip, ending with the difficulties of getting a New York theater. The children listened, not really understanding, but extremely interested, nevertheless.

When Irene and I had finished our account, Steve turned to me and said, "But when is the play going to New York, Daddy?"

"I guess you weren't paying attention," I said. "I just told you—we closed down in Philadelphia."

"Oh, I was paying attention," he said. "But what I want to know is—why can't you still take the play to New York? That's why you wrote it, isn't it?"

He had the right idea. I had to laugh. "Look, Steve. Sometimes a show just isn't quite good enough for New York. Not enough people like it, and you don't make any money, so you just fold up."

Big tears welled up in Steve's eyes and started rolling down his cheeks. "That's not fair to you, after you worked so hard," he said.

"Well, it's nothing to cry about," I told him. "It happens all the time in show business. Some plays are hits, but most aren't."

"But now you don't have any money," he said.

"What do you mean?"

"Well, you just said you didn't make any. That's why the show closed."

"Of course we have money," said Irene. (She must have had some under the mattress that I didn't know about.) "If the show had been a hit, that would have been just extra money. But we still have enough to get along on, and a nice house, and plenty of food, and lots of toys, and some still on their way—"

"If they ever get here," sighed Andy.

"Your mother's right," I told Steve, raising my glass of 1956 California champagne (a good year) in a toast. "This is Thanksgiving, and we should all be grateful for what we have."

"That's the way I look at it," said Grace philosophically. "Besides, it never does any good to cry about the past. You should just concentrate on the future. I'm sure, Arthur, you got a lot of valuable experience putting on the play this year, and even if it didn't make a million dollars, what you learned will be a big help with the next one you write."

"How soon will that be?" asked Steve eagerly, his face brightening.

"Well, probably not very soon," I explained. "It takes a while to write a whole play. You don't just do it overnight."

"We did!" said Steve, quite seriously. "Andy and I wrote a whole play one night when you were gone. We'll give it to you, Daddy, for a present. You can put it on in New York, so you don't have to wait to write a new one."

I was overwhelmed. "I'd like to read it," I said.

"Oh, you don't have to read it," said Steve. "We'll put it on for you—right now. Come on, Andy, let's get ready."

They disappeared into the living room, where they had a conference in muffled tones about the script. Then they called the three of us in.

"The name of our play is *Peter Pan*," announced Steve.

"It's a very commercial title," I said. "I like it so far."

"This is going to be *our* version of *Peter Pan*," said Steve.

"Yeah, it's much better the way we do it," added Andy.

Steve said, "Andy will play Peter. I'll be Captain Hook. Nanny, you be Tinker Bell. And Lucky can play Nana, the dog."

"Who's going to be the crocodile?" piped up Andy.

"Gee, I forgot about that," said Steve. "What about Harriet?"

"You'd better not bother Harriet," said Irene. "She has enough to do with the dishes."

"Well, we can't put on *Peter Pan* without a crocodile," said Steve.

"I've got a good idea," said Andy. He levelled his brown, saucer-like eyes at me, and frankly, he had me worried. "I know who can play the big bad ferocious crocodile."

"Who?" asked Steve.

"Yeah, who?" I said nervously.

"Our new cat!" exclaimed Andy.

"Thank God for the cat," I said. You have no idea how relieved I was that Andy didn't want *me* to play the crocodile.

"What did you say?" asked Andy.

"I said that's perfect type-casting," I replied elatedly, settling back on the sofa with Irene to enjoy the performance.

And enjoy it we did. It was a fine play, and it seemed to have a lot of possibilities. When it was over, I thanked its authors for donating the dramatic rights to me, and gave them each a quarter advance. It would have been cheap at twice the price.

Of course, their play was a little rough for Broadway in its present form, but, as I explained to Steve and Andy later, when we were tucking them into their beds, "Plays aren't written, boys —they're rewritten."

"Well, I don't know when I'll have time to rewrite it," said Steve, with a yawn. "I have to play with Bobby Wayne in the morning. And in the afternoon I have to play football with Billy Ziering."

"There's no hurry," I assured him.

"Yeah, what's the difference?" said Andy. "We probably can't get a theater, anyway."

Set in Linotype Electra
Format by Steven King
Manufactured by The Haddon Craftsmen, Inc.
Published by HARPER *&* BROTHERS, *New York*